Let It Be Me

A play

Carey Jane Hardy

Samuel French — London
New York - Toronto - Hollywood

LET IT BE ME

First produced by the Lichfield Players at the Friary
School Theatre, Lichfield on 11th April 2001 with the
following cast:

Amy Flint	Julia Butler
Sylvia	Audrey Hall
Kate	Rosemary Bodger
Trixie	Adrienne Swallow
Colin	Brian Asbury
Gregory Roberts	Phil Shaw

Directed by Chris Stanley

Subsequently produced by the Moorpool Players at
Moorpool Hall, Harborne, Birmingham on 20th
November 2001 with the following cast:

Amy Flint	Carey Jane Hardy
Sylvia	Tricia Martin
Kate	Norma Mason
Trixie	Joyce Williams
Colin	Lionel Martin
Gregory Roberts	Phil Saleh

Directed by John Healey

CHARACTERS

Amy Flint, 39
Sylvia, Amy's aunt, 60s
Kate, Amy's friend, late 30s
Trixie, Sylvia's friend and neighbour, late 50s
Colin, Amy's cousin
Gregory Roberts, an antiquarian bookseller, 50s

The action takes place in the living-room of Sylvia's house

Time — 1999

SYNOPSIS OF SCENES

ACT I

SCENE 1 Afternoon
SCENE 2 Morning, two weeks later
SCENE 3 A Saturday evening a month later

ACT II

SCENE 1 A Saturday afternoon some weeks later
SCENE 2 A few minutes later

AUTHOR'S STIPULATION

When Sylvia slaps Amy in Act II Scene 1 it is vital that this be real and not a contrived theatrical slap that stops short of contact. The audience needs to be shocked by the full force of this event. A near miss would mean that the dramatic effect of the scene and what follows would be completely destroyed.

Carey Jane Hardy

This play is dedicated
to the Moorpool Players
and to Helen with love

ACT 1

Scene 1

The living-room of Sylvia's house. Afternoon

The room is modest, light and restful. DL, *a staircase can be seen leading to an upper floor.* UL *is a door leading to the kitchen. In the back wall* C *is a door leading to the hall.* R *is a window looking out on the garden. The back wall* L *is covered by a large bookcase boasting many books, not expensive nor new but interesting. Indeed the room suggests a love of literature but not always the money with which to indulge it. There is an armchair* DS *of the bookcase.* UC *is a sofa, in front of which is a small coffee table. There is a sideboard by the wall* R *with more books on it. Against the wall* DR *is a desk on which there are a telephone, blotter and writing materials. Also in the room there is a CD player with a selection of CDs. On the back of the desk chair is Sylvia's cardigan*

When the Curtain *rises Kate is sitting on the sofa intent on reading an article in a glossy magazine. Kate is in her late thirties, attractive, stylish, and with a childish desire to be spoilt which is at times both endearing and annoying to those around her*

The telephone rings. Kate ignores it, but as it persists she looks up at it, looks at her watch, and then gets up to answer it

Kate (*into the phone*) Hallo? ... No, she's just popped out for a while. Can I take a message? ... Well, well, if it isn't Colin. How could I not have recognized that voice? How are you? ... It's Kate. ... Kate! You know, good friend Kate? Life and soul of the party Kate? The one you stood up on that date three years ago Kate? Yes, that's right. Kate. ... What? Appendicitis? ... Well of course, I thought at the time it must have been something serious. I'm not "stood up" for anything trivial as a general rule. Still it's nice to have that little matter cleared up, isn't it? One's always curious. ... Yes, I'm fine. Please don't worry. I soon found another date. ... Yes, I'm sure you did. ... No, as I said, she's just popped out. I'm babysitting. ... No, the baby's asleep. No, you didn't interrupt anything. I was just reading a fascinating article about men. Not that it doesn't tell me anything I didn't already know. Anyway, I'll tell her you rang, shall I? She will be sorry to have missed you. After all, you don't ring very often, do you? Can I take a message? ... What? ... An antiquarian? ... Oh, right. Yes,

I'll tell her. Bye-bye. ... Kate. ... Yes, Kate. ... Yes, nice talking to you too. (*She puts down the telephone, obviously disgruntled. She sits down and picks up the magazine*) Men! I could tell you a thing or two about men. (*She continues to read. Muttering under her breath*) Appendicitis! I hope it perforated!

Amy (*off*) Hallo. I'm back.

Kate Hallo!

Amy enters from the hall. She is approaching forty and is attractive in a faded sort of way. She does not have the time to take much trouble with her appearance, and there are hints that she is desperately tired by life and trying to hold back the tiredness. But at this moment she is happy and excited by her outing. She is carrying a couple of carrier bags which she puts down on the sofa. She takes off her jacket

Amy Everything all right?

Kate Fine. She's sleeping like a baby.

Amy Oh good. It was kind of you, Kate. I do appreciate it.

Kate Did you have a good time?

Amy Wonderful.

Kate Buy anything?

Amy I'm afraid I did.

Kate Naughty. Let's see.

Amy unpacks her carrier bags, producing a few hardback second-hand books

Kate (*not impressed*) Oh. Lovely.

Amy Aren't they.

Kate Sweetheart, why don't you ever treat yourself?

Amy But I just have.

Kate No, I mean really treat yourself. Buy yourself something fun to wear. Get yourself a lipstick, a new pair of shoes. Splash out on a facial. Go mad. Get some sparkle.

Amy But look at these. One of them is a first edition. And it wasn't very expensive.

Kate Next time you want to go shopping, I'll come with you. Ask Trixie to babysit, and I'll look after you. We'll have a ball. It will do you good.

Amy But this does me good, Kate. It really does. You know how I love browsing in bookshops.

Kate Listen. I'm going to leave you this magazine. Read it. Get some ideas. Glow a little.

Amy Hardly my style, Kate.

During the following, Amy dusts her new books and puts them on shelves, humming to herself as she works. Kate watches her

Kate Do you ever get time to read these books?

Amy Of course. What else are books for?

Kate (*rising and moving to the window*) Oh, I don't know. It's just that sometimes people have books as a sort of adornment to their home. It's like those show homes. Nice book shelf in corner with soft lighting. One or two books placed artistically at an angle next to bronze statue of girl on a dolphin. Then when you look closer you see that the leather bound books with improving titles are actually cardboard boxes without any pages to turn. They're just to create an effect.

Amy I really don't see the point of that. If I wanted ornaments I'd buy ornaments. I love books so I read books.

Kate You always were one for reading. You're the only person I know who really has read *War and Peace*.

Amy Only once.

Kate I haven't even seen the film.

Amy You'll have to get it out on video sometime.

Kate Don't think I will thanks. Watching *War and Peace* is not exactly my idea of a quiet night in.

Amy Sorry.

Kate Don't be. (*She picks up a book—*Ivanhoe—*from the small pile on the sideboard*) Hey, look at this.

Amy What?

Kate Is this a joke? The pages really don't open. They're all stuck together. Look.

Amy I know. Isn't it gorgeous?

Kate Gorgeous? I'd take it back. Get a refund.

Amy I picked it up in the second-hand bookshop a few weeks ago. I just couldn't resist it. The pages are uncut which means of course that no-one has read it. So I'll be the very first.

Kate So what? If you bought new books then you'd always be the first to read them.

Amy It's not the same. Look at the date. 1901. The beginning of the century. In all this time I'm the first person to read it.

Kate What will you do? Cut the pages?

Amy Eventually. But then after I'd brought it I just had this thought that the book might be more valuable like that. I wouldn't want to deface it or devalue it.

Kate You mean I might be holding a fortune in my hands?

Amy Well, probably not a fortune. If so, someone other than me would have picked it up long ago. But you never know. I rang Colin and he suggested showing it to an expert. Just to get an opinion. Colin knows someone who deals in antiquarian books. He said we should get his opinion.

Kate (*sitting on the sofa*) Oh, that's what it was all about.

Amy What?

Kate Sorry, I should have said. Colin rang while you were out. He mentioned this antiquarian thingamy. I didn't know what he was talking about, but I wasn't going to give Colin the satisfaction of knowing that. Anyway, he's said he's spoken to him and he'll be in touch with you. He was going to bring him round himself, but he thought it would be easier just to give the chap your name and address and let him come when he had the chance.

Amy Oh, I see.

Kate And it lets Colin off the hook, doesn't it? How is he, by the way? I haven't seen him forever. (*She hands the book to Amy*)

Amy Neither have I. (*She moves to the desk and puts the book down*)

Kate I hear he had appendicitis.

Amy (*puzzled*) Did he?

Kate My mistake. Perhaps it wasn't appendicitis. Perhaps it was a guilty conscience.

Amy He has nothing to feel guilty about, Kate. He'd be here if I needed him. I just don't need him.

Kate Who does?

Aunt Sylvia's voice is heard from upstairs

Sylvia (*off*) Amy? Amy?

Kate The baby awakes.

Amy Oh dear. I was hoping she would sleep for a while longer. (*She goes to the foot of the stairs to meet Sylvia*)

Sylvia enters, descending the stairs. She is in her sixties but looks older. She carries the restless, distracted, worried air of someone who is battling with loss of memory. She has just woken from sleep, which accentuates her distress. She appears thin and vulnerable for she does not eat well

Sylvia Amy? Where's Amy?

Amy It's all right, Aunt Sylvia. Amy's at school. She'll be home later.

Sylvia Oh, yes, of course. At school. She'll be home soon. I must get her tea.

Amy Don't worry, I'll do that. There's plenty of time. She won't be home yet.

Sylvia (*pacing up and down*) Won't she? Oh dear. The days seem so long. Do we have cake? Chocolate cake. She likes chocolate cake. It's her favourite. Shall I make her a cake? I think I'll make her a cake.

Amy I made one yesterday, Aunt Sylvia. It's in the tin. All ready.

Sylvia Oh good. How kind. Amy will be so pleased. She likes chocolate cake. I'll go and wait in the garden so I can see her when she comes.
Amy She won't be home for a while yet. Why don't you try and sleep a little longer? I'll call you when she comes.
Sylvia No. No I must wait in the garden. I don't want to miss her.
Amy Please.
Sylvia I want to wait in the garden.
Amy (*after a pause*) Put a cardigan on. It's rather cold today. (*She picks up the cardigan from the back of the desk chair*)

Sylvia exits into the hall

Kate Will she be all right?
Amy For a while. Hopefully she won't stay out for long. She'll think of something else and come in again. Just as long as she doesn't go wandering off.
Kate Does she often try?
Amy No. Actually it's been difficult to entice her out of the house for months. She feels safe as long as she's here.
Kate No place like home!
Amy At least it's familiar to her. Outside everything seems — well, different to her, threatening. She hasn't even been over to Trixie's for months, and you know what good friends they've always been.
Kate Surely she'd know where she was at Trixie's?
Amy Perhaps she would when she got there. But the walk up the road is a nightmare to her, even though it's only a few doors away.
Kate When I think about all those Bridge evenings.
Amy Long gone. Trixie still hosts them, of course, but Sylvia doesn't go. It was strange in the beginning. I think Sylvia realized before any of us did that she just couldn't keep track of the game any more. So she just stopped going. Perhaps even now Trixie's house reminds her too much of a time when she was — different.
Kate How awful. It must be worse when you know yourself that you're losing ground.
Amy (*moving to the window and looking out*) Yes. But then I wonder how much she does remember. Her mind wanders so far that I have a job keeping up with it. That's what I meant about wandering off. How can you reassure someone when you don't know what they're thinking or where they are?
Kate I don't know how you manage.
Amy Because I have to manage. Besides, it's not all bad. She has her good days.
Kate Colin should come more often.

Amy Why?
Kate To take a share of the responsibility?
Amy Aunt Sylvia is my responsibility, not Colin's.
Kate She's his aunt too.
Amy Yes, but it's different, isn't it? She brought me up. Colin was just an occasional visitor. He's her nephew, but I'm the daughter she never had. She and I are a family unit. You know that. It's always been like that.

The doorbell rings

Kate I'd say speak of the devil. But it can't be him.
Amy I doubt it.
Kate I'll go. You keep watch.
Amy Thanks, Kate.

Kate exits into the hall

Kate's and Gregory Roberts's voices come from the hall. Amy's attention remains on the garden

Kate and Gregory Roberts enter. Gregory is in his fifties, distinguished-looking without being ostentatious, for he is sometimes unsure of himself and shy of company. His quietness and kindness have made him a very astute observer of human nature

Kate I think this is Colin's antiquarian.
Amy (*turning*) Oh.
Gregory (*holding out his hand to Amy*) Hallo, I'm Gregory Roberts. I do hope you don't mind me just dropping in. Your cousin told me I'd be likely to find you in and since I was in the neighbourhood ...
Amy (*a little flustered, half keeping her eye on her aunt through the window*) Yes, of course. I mean, not at all. It's very kind of you to come. I must admit I hadn't really expected you so soon. But thank you. Please do sit down.

Gregory wanders over to the bookcase

(*To Kate*) Kate, would you mind. I can't see ...
Kate Of course. I'll go and find her.

Kate exits into the hall

Gregory You have quite a collection here.
Amy Not really a collection. I know nothing about books as collector's items. I love to read. I always have. And I love the atmosphere of small second-hand bookshops. So I browse when I get an opportunity, and occasionally I treat myself.

Gregory What do you treat yourself to?

Amy Anything that takes my fancy. And that could be for any obscure reason: the title, the feel of the book, something that catches my eye. Sometimes it's the inscription. The real fascination of second-hand books is the thought of the people who have read them before me. But this one — (*she picks up* Ivanhoe *from the desk*) this one fascinated me because despite its age no-one could have read it before. You see, some of the pages are still uncut.

Gregory Ah, this is the one you wanted me to see?

Amy Yes, if you wouldn't mind.

Amy hands Ivanhoe *to Gregory*

Gregory Not at all. I … Ah. *Ivanhoe*. Are you a fan of Walter Scott?

Amy If I'm in the mood. *Ivanhoe* is a particular favourite. (*She sits on the sofa*)

Gregory I don't suppose you have that much time for reading now. (*He sits in the armchair*)

Amy At night mostly. I have to be watchful. Reading passes the time when it's difficult to sleep. Don't you think it's a lovely volume?

Gregory Yes, it is. Macmillan and Co. Limited. 1901. The beginning of a new century. And here we are at the end of it.

Amy Exactly. A whole century. And the pages still uncut. So in all that time no-one has read it.

Gregory Also something of a waste, when you think about it. No inscription. It makes you wonder if it has ever belonged to anyone.

Amy Well, it belongs to me now. There's a printed dedication from the publisher.

Gregory (*reading*) "This Edition is dedicated by the publisher to the Hon. Mrs Maxwell Scott of Abbotsford and her children, Great Granddaughter and Great Great Grandchildren of the Author."

Amy Isn't that something! I wonder what Scott would have thought if he could have looked into the future and seen that dedication in a copy of his novel. Generations of his family, a part of himself, that he could never have known.

Gregory No more than you and I would think if we looked into our own future. We presume that generations will come after us, but we can guess little about them.

Amy But it fascinates me, doesn't it you? To be part of something like that. An ever-flowing stream.

Gregory Do you know, you remind me so much of myself. Put an old book in my hand and I feel that there is so much more than the printed page between its covers. You know, the very first time ——

The voices of Sylvia and Kate, off, interrupt Gregory. He places the book on the coffee table and rises

Sylvia Amy, Amy.

Sylvia enters, followed by Kate

Kate Sorry, she was looking for Amy. I thought it best to bring her in.

Amy gets up and tries to comfort Sylvia

Sylvia Where is Amy? She should be home by now. They said she'd gone somewhere. Where was it now?

Kate School. She's at school.

Sylvia School. That's right. (*To Amy*) Is that right? Is she at school, again?

Amy Yes, that's right. Everything's all right, Aunt Sylvia. Amy's quite safe.

Sylvia She's away for so long. So long. I want her to come home. Something's not right, not right. I should go up to the school and find her. It's not like her to be late. (*She turns and sees Gregory*) Who is this?

Gregory (*holding out his hand*) I'm Gregory Roberts. I've come to look at ——

Sylvia Is Amy all right?

There is a pause. Gregory looks puzzled

Amy Amy's quite well, Aunt Sylvia. I promise that there's nothing to worry about. You'll see her soon.

Sylvia But how will she get home? I should be there for her. I always meet her at the corner and then we walk home together. She shouldn't be left to walk alone. Not a little girl like that.

Kate Look, I'll walk up and meet her, shall I? (*She raises her eyes at Amy*) Just to make sure.

Sylvia Oh, yes, that would be good. But surely I should go? She'd expect me. She might not know you. Who are you?

Kate Amy's friend. Amy's friend Kate. You remember me.

Sylvia (*in sudden recognition*) Kate? Are you Kate? Of course, of course. Kate.

Kate I'll put the kettle on first. Come and show me where everything is.

Sylvia Where's Amy?

Kate ushers Sylvia out to the kitchen. There is an embarrassed silence

Gregory She seems very fond of the child.

Amy Yes, she is. Amy is everything to her. (*She moves to the window*)
Gregory How old is she?
Amy Aunt Sylvia?
Gregory No, no, I meant Amy.
Amy (*after a pause, looking out of the window*) She'll be forty next birthday.
(*She turns to him*) Forgive me. I should have introduced myself. You see,
I am Amy Flint.
Gregory You are Amy? But ... (*He moves to her*)
Amy My aunt is — well — not always quite herself.
Gregory I see.
Amy (*moving to the sofa and sitting*) As far as she is concerned, Amy is still
a child. She seems unable to remember that I grew up. Even in her
confusion, she is curiously adamant about some things. This one in
particular. To remind her in any way that Amy is not a child causes her great
distress. She brought me up, you see. It's as if she feels safer in that time
frame. In the end it seems — kinder — to ...
Gregory Pretend?
Amy Not pretend exactly. Just travel back in time with her, to a certain time
and place where she feels safe. And she is remarkably accurate in those
memories. She did used to walk down to the corner shop to meet me from
school. And we walked home together and had tea at the kitchen table. All
those little details are still intact. At least, for the present. It's just that the
future ...
Gregory It must be hard.
Amy It must be harder still for her. So I don't complain.
Gregory No. I'm sure you don't. But it must be strange.
Amy To live out my childhood all over again? Yes, it's very strange. Except
of course, that it isn't me. It's someone else. Another Amy.
Gregory And who is the other Amy? (*He sits on the sofa*)
Amy What?
Gregory I'm sorry. It just occurred to me that when your aunt asks you about
Amy, who does she think you are?
Amy I really don't think she knows.
Gregory That must be the hardest part of all.

*There is a pause. Amy looks at Gregory, surprised, perhaps, and moved that
he should seem to understand so quickly*

Amy I believe that she still feels safe with me. That she recognizes me as
someone who cares for her and cares about her, and about Amy. Which of
course is true.
Gregory It seems such a waste.
Amy But that's just the point, you see. My aunt is suffering from a wasting

disease. Not of the body, but of the mind. All her memories, slowly, are being lost. Yes, I call that a terrible waste. (*Pause*) I'm sorry, this is not what you came for.

Gregory (*standing, embarrassed*) No, I'm sorry. I don't even know you. I shouldn't be prying.

Amy I don't think you are prying. Really I don't. I rarely talk about the situation. I suppose I feel it's disloyal to my aunt to talk about her to other people. But sometimes it's necessary to explain. Somehow I felt able to explain it to you. It was good of you to come today. I'm sorry you found me — somewhat distracted.

Gregory Not at all. I found you ...

Amy (*laughing*) Please don't feel you have to complete the sentence. "Not at all" would have done.

Gregory (*sitting again*) I found you quite charming.

Amy (*embarrassed*) I think Kate is making tea. Will you have some? There'll be chocolate cake.

Gregory My favourite.

Amy Amy's too.

Gregory Where were we?

Amy (*picking up the book again and handing it to Gregory*) Indulging in old books.

Gregory Oh yes, of course. And the ever-flowing stream.

Amy And our place in it.

Gregory (*looking at Amy and smiling*) You mentioned that your aunt brought you up. Do you remember your parents?

Amy No. They were killed in a road accident when I was only a baby. Aunt Sylvia was babysitting.

Gregory Oh I see. So you became her continuation.

Amy Yes. She was looking after me when the accident happened, so she just carried on looking after me. She took her sister's place and became my mother.

Gregory But you don't call her "Mother"?

Amy She never encouraged it. I think she liked to be truthful. She already had a legitimate claim to me. She was my mother's sister. She became my legal guardian. She told me about my parents when I asked her. But our relationship was never threatened. We belonged together. We had no-one else.

Gregory What about Colin?

Amy Colin is my cousin. He came to tea and she baked more chocolate cakes. Then he went home. They always got on fine. But Colin was her brother's son, with a home and family of his own. I was her girl. All hers. That was the difference.

Gregory He didn't mention your aunt. At least — he mentioned her — but not ...

Amy Not her problems.
Gregory I suppose there was no reason to. It's none of my business after all.
Amy Colin is not a frequent visitor. And Sylvia has her good days. It could
be that he is not always aware of — changes.
Gregory But now that things are — well — more difficult, shouldn't he help
out more? Be here more often?

Kate enters with a tea tray, unseen for a moment by Amy

Amy You're beginning to sound like Kate. For some reason she is always
so down on Colin. But Colin doesn't live here. I do.
Kate You need a break. (*She places the tray on the coffee table*)
Amy I don't need a break. (*She rises and moves to the bookcase*)
Gregory (*rising*) Do you ever get out?
Amy Of course, I go to bookshops. (*She holds up some books*) Don't you
remember?
Kate You go out for less than an hour at a time. And you only agree to go
if Sylvia is asleep.
Gregory Can you leave her?
Amy Of course not. Kate stays with her while I'm out. (*To Kate*) And I
enjoyed it very much and I'm very grateful. Now, let's have tea. Where's
Aunt Sylvia?
Kate She was bringing the plates. Is that allowed?

Amy gets up and moves to the kitchen door

Amy Are you all right, Aunt Sylvia?
Sylvia (*off*) Yes, of course. I'm just coming. Don't fuss so.

Sylvia enters with plates

During the following, Amy stands by the door, watching the scene

(*Patting Amy's hand as she passes her*) Oh, we have guests. How nice. You
didn't tell me we had visitors. Amy will be pleased to see you. (*She comes
forward and seats herself on the sofa, playing the perfect hostess. Were it
not for her comments about Amy she would appear perfectly lucid. During
the following she serves tea with complete alacrity*) May I offer you tea?
Gregory Why, thank you, yes. (*He sits on the sofa*)
Sylvia Milk and sugar?
Gregory Please.
Sylvia How many spoons?
Gregory Sorry?

Sylvia (*kindly and patiently*) Sugar? How many spoons of sugar?
Gregory Oh just one, thank you.
Sylvia There you are. (*She hands him his cup*) And Kate. How nice of you
to come. No sugar for you. I know how you like it. You young girls are
always watching your weight. (*She hands Kate her cup*) But you must have
cake. Will you both have cake?
Gregory Thank you.
Kate Yes, please. (*She sits on the desk chair*)

*Sylvia cuts the cake and serves it, then pours another cup of tea and turns to
Amy*

Sylvia Come and sit down, dear.

Amy sits in an armchair

Don't let your tea get cold. And I know you'll have cake. Chocolate. Your
favourite. That's it. Oh, isn't this nice. Just like old times. (*She turns to
Gregory*) You must forgive me, but I can't recall your name.
Gregory That's quite all right. I'm Gregory Roberts. Colin asked me if I
would come and look at one of Am ... at a book for Miss Flint.
Sylvia Oh, yes, we have lots of books, don't we, dear?
Amy Yes, Aunt Sylvia. I found one the other day, an old book, with its pages
still uncut. Colin suggested that Mr Roberts have a look at it.
Sylvia Books are your subject, are they?
Gregory Yes, in a way. My work and my hobby combined.
Sylvia Oh, it must be lovely to know a lot about something. I often feel I know
very little about anything. (*She laughs. Pause. A puzzled look crosses her
face, as though she is trying to remember something. But then she turns to
Gregory again, making an effort*) Do you have a shop of your own?
Gregory Well, I spend quite a lot of time lecturing. All very dull to some,
I'm afraid. But I run a couple of antiquarian bookshops in Hay-on-Wye.
Sylvia Oh, yes, how nice. Hay-on-Wye. Pretty place. I haven't been there
for years and years. We must have a run out there sometime. We don't get
out very much these days ... Did you say you knew Colin?
Gregory Yes, that's right. He stands between me and the tax man. I may
know a lot about books, but Colin is far better at cooking them!
Sylvia What?
Gregory I'm sorry. I was being flippant.
Kate Trying to make a joke, Sylvia.
Gregory Colin sorts out my tax returns for me. Something I'm not very good
at.
Kate I knew there was a purpose in this world even for Colin.

Sylvia A clever boy, Colin. Always was. Good with figures. (*She leans forward confidentially to Gregory*) And I don't just mean arithmetic, either. (*She giggles*)

Kate sniffs

(*Reacting to Kate*) Of course, Kate pretends to disagree with me. But she's always had a soft spot for Colin, really.

Kate Oh, have I, indeed? Well, it must be my age or something but that spot is turning into a corn — distinctly hard.

Sylvia Dear Kate. You always gave him a difficult time. He'll settle down and see sense one of these days.

Kate Miracles may happen. But who says I want them to?

Sylvia I do! (*She leans forward and picks up the teapot*) More tea, anyone?

Gregory Thank you, no. I really ought to be going.

Sylvia Oh, please don't go just yet. It's nearly five o'clock. Amy will be home soon. She'd be sorry to miss you.

Gregory Perhaps … (*He looks at Amy*) Perhaps I could visit Amy another time.

Sylvia Another time? Why of course. You would be most welcome any time. Though Amy is at school during the day.

Gregory Yes. I'll remember that. (*He gets up and holds out his hand to Sylvia*) Please don't get up. Thank you for tea. The chocolate cake was indeed delicious.

Sylvia I'm so glad. (*She leans forward and whispers*) It's Amy's favourite. I shall tell her she has a fellow admirer.

Amy rises

Gregory (*glancing at Amy*) She certainly does. (*He moves to Amy*) Perhaps I could take the book with me.

Amy Of course. (*She fetches the book and gives it to Gregory*) Thank you for being — so kind.

Gregory Not kind at all. I'll let you know about the book.

Kate I must be going too. Thanks for tea, Sylvia. If you hear from Colin, remind him I'm alive. (*She kisses Sylvia's cheek*)

Sylvia looks surprised at the kiss. She is beginning to retreat again and has not made sense of Kate's last remark

I'll see Mr Roberts out. I know the way.

Gregory (*shaking hands with Amy*) Goodbye.

Amy Goodbye.

Kate and Gregory exit into the hall

Amy remains US *near the door*

Sylvia It was nice to have visitors, dear. But you might have mentioned they were coming. I'd have made a little more effort. After all, I don't see many people now. Apart from Trixie of course. But Trixie is hardly a visitor. We should have had two kinds of cake. And sandwiches. Cucumber sandwiches. I could have put on my best dress. What a nice man he seemed. What did you say his name was?

Amy Roberts. Gregory Roberts. (*She moves to the window*)

Sylvia (*puzzled*) Should I know him?

Amy No. Neither of us had met him before today.

Sylvia He hasn't been here before?

Amy No.

Sylvia His face looked — familiar.

Amy Did it?

Sylvia It was a nice face.

Amy Yes, it was.

Sylvia But I can't remember when … (*She shakes her head*) Oh, I don't know. Faces — confuse me.

Amy (*sitting on the sofa*) I really don't think you should worry. Perhaps he just reminded you of someone. But he hasn't been to the house before.

Sylvia He said he knew someone …

Amy Colin.

Sylvia Yes, that's right. (*Pause*) Does he mean our Colin?

Amy Yes, our Colin. I asked Colin if he knew anyone who could give me an opinion on a book. And Colin recommended Gregory Roberts.

Sylvia A book?

Amy A book by Walter Scott.

Sylvia Do I know him?

Amy Walter Scott?

Sylvia Yes.

Amy No, Aunt Sylvia. Walter Scott died a long, long time ago.

Sylvia So he's never been to the house either?

Amy (*to herself*) Not this century anyway.

Sylvia What?

Amy No. He hasn't been here. Just his books. He died in 1832.

Sylvia And where are we now?

Amy 1999. The end of the Millennium.

Sylvia What?

Amy End of a century. End of a thousand years.

Sylvia All that time. I didn't know. Was I asleep?

Amy Don't worry, darling. You and I haven't been here for very much of
   it.
Sylvia (*still puzzled*) How old are we, then?
Amy (*after a pause*) As old or as young as we feel.

Sylvia leans back her head and closes her eyes

Sylvia Amy will be home soon. That will be nice.

Amy turns and looks at Sylvia

CURTAIN

SCENE 2

The same. Two weeks later. Morning

*There is a boxed jigsaw puzzle and the beginnings of a shopping list on the
desk. Sylvia's dressing-gown is on the back of the sofa*

When the CURTAIN *rises, Sylvia, still wearing her night-dress, is standing by
the bookcase carefully taking books out of the bookshelf, putting them in
piles, then putting them back. Growing tired of her task she turns and
wanders around the room*

Amy (*off*) Aunt Sylvia?

*Passing the desk, Sylvia knocks the jigsaw box on to the floor. The pieces spill
out. Annoyed with herself, she bends down and begins to pick up the pieces.
She stops, noticing something about a piece of jigsaw; she then looks at other
pieces, one by one. Very painfully, she tries to do the jigsaw on the floor*

   Aunt Sylvia?

Amy enters from the kitchen. She is wearing a cardigan

Amy Aunt Sylvia, do come and finish your breakfast. You'll fade away ...
   What are you doing?
Sylvia Somebody has cut up the picture.
Amy What?
Sylvia The picture of this woman. Look. Here are bits of her face. All cut up.
   Why should anyone do such a thing?
Amy It's a jigsaw, Aunt Sylvia.

Sylvia It's a shame.

Amy It's a jigsaw. Don't you remember? You put all the pieces together to make the picture.

Sylvia That's what I'm trying to do. What a mess. What a shame. Cutting up the picture. I shall have to speak to Amy. Whatever made her do it?

Amy Do come and finish breakfast. Then I'll help you dress.

Sylvia But I must do this.

Amy Why not have breakfast first?

Sylvia Her poor face. Her poor face. Oh look. Part of her dress. All the bits of blue must be part of her dress.

Amy I could find your blue dress. Would you like to put it on today?

Sylvia All these bits of blue. Like the sky.

The doorbell rings

Amy That will be Trixie. She's come for our shopping list. Why don't you come and finish your breakfast? Please.

Amy exits into the hall

Sylvia continues to exclaim over the jigsaw, very slowly putting little bits together here and there on the carpet

(*Off*) I haven't finished the list, I'm afraid. I'm trying to persuade Aunt Sylvia to get dressed.

Amy enters with Trixie, who is in her late fifties, well-dressed, extrovert and capable

Trixie Hallo, Sylvia, how are you today?

Amy It's Trixie, Aunt Sylvia.

Sylvia (*still hunting for bits of jigsaw*) Such a pity.

Trixie What is? (*She sits on the sofa*) What's the matter, Sylvia?

Sylvia (*looking up at Trixie*) Did you do this?

Trixie I confess nothing. Nothing at all. Not without speaking to my solicitor first. What's the problem?

Amy Try to remember, Aunt Sylvia. It's a jigsaw. A sort of game. It's supposed to be in pieces. You put them together to make the picture. Then you take them apart again.

Sylvia What a very strange thing to do.

Trixie You have a point there, Sylvia. (*To Amy*) I'm in no rush. Sit down and finish your list.

Amy You must be cold, Aunt Sylvia. Would you at least put on a dressing-gown or a cardigan?

Sylvia Look. Her hand. One of her hands. Cut off.
Amy (*in almost a whisper*) It's just a jigsaw. Just a picture.

Trixie looks at Amy. Seeing her tension, she gets down on the floor beside Sylvia. She takes Sylvia's hands in her own

Trixie Do you remember our Scrabble evenings, Sylvia?
Sylvia (*looking up at Trixie, seemingly surprised to see her*) Scrabble?
Trixie All those letters. Little bits of words. You were a champion. And I remember that time you won the game with your last letter, because you tripled your score. And I was so cross that I knocked the board over and all the letters were scattered.
Sylvia Letters?
Trixie But the words were still there. Ready to be made all over again, the next time.
Sylvia Next time?

Trixie persuades Sylvia to her feet. Amy picks up Sylvia's dressing-gown. She and Trixie help Sylvia to put the dressing-gown on, then gently sit her down on the sofa

During the following, Amy exits into the kitchen, returning with a bowl of cereal and a spoon

Trixie No harm was done at all. It was just a game. Even though I pretended to be so angry. It was fun. I loved those evenings. You and me and a gin and tonic. And that wicked mind of yours. A letter here, a letter there, and double your score. Sometimes I thought, I feel lucky tonight, I shall win the game. But then in you'd come, with a z or a q and produce a gem. You were a cunning player, Sylvia.
Sylvia Was I?

Amy gives the bowl of cereal to Trixie. Trixie carefully coaxes Sylvia to open her mouth, and feeds her like a child during the following. Amy watches Trixie and Sylvia for a moment and then goes to the desk to finish her shopping list

Trixie You were the same with crosswords. Always solved the clues before me. Mind you, I think you cheated.
Sylvia Cheated?
Trixie All those dictionaries. Crossword encyclopaedias.
Sylvia Not cheating. No, not cheating. That was … That was … What was it? Something. Looking … Underneath … Looking … Searching …
Trixie Research?

Sylvia (*smiling, a gleam in her eye*) Yes, Yes. Research. For words. Very important, words. I never cheated. (*She takes the bowl and spoon from Trixie and continues to feed herself*)

There is a moment of quiet. Trixie watches Sylvia carefully chewing her cereal. Amy is absorbed in her list. Then Sylvia catches sight of the jigsaw and suddenly begins to weep quietly

Her hands. Her poor hands. They shouldn't have done it. That lovely dress. All gone. All gone.
Amy (*getting up quickly and moving to the stairs*) Could you put the jigsaw away, Trixie, please. I'll get her clothes.

Amy exits up the stairs

Trixie Out of sight, out of mind. Is that it? (*She kneels down and gathers up some of the jigsaw pieces, putting them in the box*)

Sylvia sees what Trixie is doing and stops weeping but then becomes agitated. She abandons her bowl and tries to rescue some of the pieces from Trixie's hands

In the box, Sylvia. Can you put them in the box? We're tidying up for Amy.
Sylvia (*stopping*) Amy? Is Amy home already?
Trixie (*under her breath*) My mistake. (*She picks up the lid with the picture on and shows it to Sylvia*) Look, you see. All together again. Isn't she beautiful?

Sylvia takes the box from Trixie's hands and stares in wonder at the picture

Sylvia (*searching for the word*) That's ... That's ... That's ...
Trixie What?
Sylvia That's better. Yes. Better. (*She rocks very gently back and forward during the following, holding the lid of the jigsaw box to herself*)

Amy enters down the stairs holding a plain button-front dress and a cardigan. She takes in the scene

Trixie takes the dress from Amy's hands and holds it out

Trixie Haven't you got anything better than this? She used to be a lady of style. What happened to her proper clothes, her suits, her blouses, her court shoes?

Amy (*fighting to keep control*) Trixie, have you any idea how long it takes Sylvia to dress in the mornings? Buttons and belts and zips confuse her. She can't remember how to fasten them. Most days I have to dress her anyway, but she gets frightened if it takes too long. She fights me, fights the clothes. She hates things over her head. It's easier to get her into simple clothes. Otherwise she'd still be in her night-dress at teatime.

Trixie Would that matter?

Amy Of course it would matter. She would never have dreamed of not getting dressed. She's always been a lady of standards. I can't let that slip.

Trixie She used to be a lady of taste but that has more than slipped. She wouldn't have been seen dead in these clothes. I certainly wouldn't. And she's only a few years older than me.

Amy She gets distressed enough with the simplest procedure. I just do everything I can to make it quicker and easier for her.

Trixie Sylvia has been my neighbour for more than thirty years. I remember her as the best-dressed woman in the road.

Amy I remember that too, Trixie. Do you think I don't? (*She holds herself tense, close to tears, trying to calm herself*)

Trixie and Amy look at each other for a moment

Trixie I'm sorry.

They look at Sylvia, still rocking and holding the lid of the jigsaw box

(*Moving to Sylvia and taking her arm*) Come with me, my friend. We're going to dress you like a queen today. (*She tries to take the box lid away from Sylvia*)

Sylvia hangs on to the lid, whimpering

Amy Let her take the picture, Trixie.

Trixie Absolutely. That can be our inspiration.

Trixie leads Sylvia to the stairs and they slowly head up them

Amy You've got your shopping to do.

Trixie I told you I was in no rush. This is something I want to do, for Sylvia.

Trixie and Sylvia exit, disappearing up the stairs

Amy (*quietly to herself*) Do you think I don't?

*Amy stands with her arms folded for a moment, her head bowed. She is so
tense that she is in danger of breaking down. Then with a great effort she pulls
herself together and looks around the room. She bends down and, very
carefully, as though still trying to control herself, gathers the remaining
jigsaw pieces tidily into the box, stands and carries the box to the desk*

The doorbell rings

Again, with great effort, Amy stands straight, then exits into the hall

We hear voices off

Amy and Gregory enter. Gregory carries Amy's copy of Ivanhoe

Gregory I'm sorry it has taken me so long. I've had your book for nearly two
weeks. It was very remiss of me. I suppose I could have telephoned but ...
Amy Oh, that's quite all right. Please don't worry. Won't you sit down.

Gregory sits in the armchair, Amy on the sofa

So what do you think?
Gregory It's a beautiful book and a treasure in itself. But, I have to admit,
it isn't really that valuable, and as for the pages being uncut ... Well, it
would not deface the book to cut them. They add no extra value to the book,
you see. So my advice would be to cut the pages and enjoy being the very
first to read it.

*Amy looks at Gregory for a moment and then gets up from the sofa and moves
towards the window. She looks out into the garden and then begins to cry.
Gregory, surprised and troubled, gets up and goes to Amy, standing behind
her*

Why, Miss Flint — Amy, what is it? I'm so sorry, I didn't realize that you
had placed so much hope in the value of the book. I thought it was just out
of interest. Please ... (*He wants to put his hands on her shoulders as he
stands behind her, but cannot quite bring himself to do so*) Would the
money have — helped so much?
Amy (*desperately trying to control herself*) No, no. It's not the money. It's
not that.
Gregory Please tell me ... What can I do? (*Again he tries to put out a hand
to her but feels utterly helpless*)
Amy I don't think I really believed the book was valuable. And if it had been?
Well, perhaps the money would have been useful, but ... No, I wouldn't
have sold it. It wasn't the money. I'm not in desperate financial need. I
would just have kept it, and treasured it.

Gregory I believed that you already treasured the book, and not for any financial reason.

Amy You're right, of course. It's just ... Oh, it's so silly. I can't explain.

Gregory Please try. If it would help.

Amy Sometimes you hold on to beliefs, dreams, treasures, call them what you like, however small and insignificant they might seem to someone else. Because for a time they make a difference. Make everything seem — worthwhile. And then something happens, something small, unexpected, and you realize that you had made a mistake, that what you held on to and believed in cannot provide the refuge you longed for. That in fact it makes no difference at all. And life is just the same as it always was. Except that it seems just a little more grey and a little more drab than it did before. And you think, "Is this it? Is this all there is?" And for a single moment the disappointment is so crushing that it seems unbearable.

There is a moment's pause. Gregory watches Amy, unable to comprehend her distress, but understanding that this goes deeper than he can see

(*Turning to him and trying to smile*) Forgive me. You simply caught me at a bad moment. I'll get over it.

Gregory Is there anything I can do? (*He watches Amy intently and with great concern during the following*)

Amy (*moving past him to sit down again*) Please don't worry. I have a habit of making mountains out of molehills. Rather childish really. I remember feeling like this before. It will pass. (*She looks up at him, realizing that he is watching*) You must think me very foolish.

Gregory Not at all.

Amy As I said. Just a bad moment. (*She stands again and looks up towards the stairs*)

Gregory (*following Amy's glance*) How are things?

Amy (*turning to him, trying to be bright and confident*) Fine. Really. (*She turns once more towards the stairs and a look of concern crosses her face*)

Gregory And your aunt. How is she?

Amy As well as can be expected. Thank you.

Gregory wanders towards the desk and sees the jigsaw

Gregory Do you enjoy jigsaws?

Amy Not particularly. It sometimes passes the time. My aunt is the jigsaw enthusiast. At least, she was. That particular one was a present from Amy some years ago. (*She suddenly realizes what she has said*) I mean — I gave it to her some years ago. It's a copy of a painting she once admired.

Gregory It must have given her a lot of pleasure.

Amy Yes it did. Once.

Gregory (*tentatively*) Amy — I was wondering. That is … I thought, perhaps — if you could get someone to stay with your aunt … I wondered if you would join me one evening. We could have a meal or see a play or … (*He turns to her somewhat helplessly*) If you would like to.

There is a pause

Amy It's very kind of you but …
Gregory Oh no, it's not out of kindness or — anything like that. I really would enjoy your company.
Amy (*smiling*) And I believe I would enjoy yours.
Gregory Then you'll come?
Amy (*after a pause*) I'd love to. But …
Gregory Don't let there be any buts. Please.
Amy I'll have to let you know. I'd need to arrange something for my aunt.
Gregory Tomorrow.
Amy I don't know. It might be difficult.
Gregory Tomorrow. Make it tomorrow.
Amy Are you always so persistent?
Gregory Only when things are important.
Amy (*smiling at his earnest manner*) Very well. Tomorrow. If I can.
Gregory About seven?
Amy I'll have to … Oh, all right. Seven.
Gregory Thank you. I'll look forward to it. So much.
Amy So will I.
Gregory Your book. (*He hands the book to her*)
Amy Oh yes. Thank you for taking the trouble to look at it. And I'm sorry for making such a scene.
Gregory Not at all. I'm sorry that it wasn't as special as you'd hoped.
Amy It still is. Really.
Gregory I do hope so. I would hate you to lose that enjoyment.
Amy It won't stay away for long.
Gregory Yes. Well, I must go. (*He moves to the hall door*)

Amy follows Gregory. They exit

Gregory (*off*) See you tomorrow.
Amy (*off*) Yes. Goodbye. Thank you for calling.

We hear the front door shut

Amy enters

Trixie (*off; from upstairs*) Here we are. All done and dusted and fit for a king.

Trixie and Sylvia enter down the stairs. Sylvia is dressed smartly and stylishly in blue, with a touch of lipstick. Trixie has the lid of the jigsaw box in her hand

Trixie What do you think?

Amy Why Aunt Sylvia, you look lovely. Really lovely. Thank you, Trixie.

Trixie It was nothing. I enjoyed it because I don't have to do it every day, and Sylvia enjoyed it because for once she wanted to play the game. I used the picture. (*She hands Amy the jigsaw lid*) We were just dressing up, that's all. Little girls love it.

Amy Sylvia isn't a little girl, Trixie.

Trixie Neither am I, but one can always dream. We were just remembering what it was like to be young and dressing up for a special reason. We played together. No patronage was implied. Now, where's that shopping list?

Amy Here. I'm bound to have forgotten something. (*She holds out the list to Trixie*)

Trixie Everyone does. (*She takes the list*) Though I suspect you forget more than most. (*She looks at the list*) You'd starve on this. Am I invited to lunch?

Amy Of course.

Trixie Then I'll use my imagination. And how are you for gin?

Amy We're fine. It depends how thirsty you are.

Trixie That depends on the queue at the checkout and who I meet on the way.

Amy Then I'd get another bottle just in case.

Trixie Fair enough. My treat, of course.

Amy Trixie? Um, I don't suppose, I mean — could you perhaps sit with Aunt Sylvia tomorrow night?

Trixie Why?

Amy I thought I'd go out.

Trixie But you never go out on Saturday evenings.

Amy Is it Saturday tomorrow?

Trixie Presumably. It usually is when it's Friday today.

Amy I'd just forgotten.

Trixie Where are you going?

Amy Oh, I don't know. He hadn't quite decided.

Trixie He?

Amy Gregory Roberts.

Trixie When did all this happen?

Amy Just now.

Trixie While we were upstairs?

Amy Yes.

Trixie Well that was fast work.

Amy (*turning suddenly, her pleasure evident*) Oh, could you, Trixie? Please?

Trixie Of course. But if this is going to be a regular thing I'd better warn you that I usually have other arrangements for Saturday evenings.

Amy Oh, thank you. Just before seven?

Trixie Just before seven. Sylvia, have me a gin and tonic poured for just before seven, all right. Now where's that list?

Amy You have it.

Trixie So I have. Goodbye.

Amy Goodbye, and thank you, Trixie.

Trixie Not at all. Just promise me one thing. Don't wear that cardigan tomorrow night.

Amy I promise.

Amy and Trixie exit into the hall

Sylvia looks carefully down at her dress, feeling the material. Then slowly and carefully she does a twirl, and then another. She laughs

Amy enters

Amy watches her aunt for a moment and then goes to her and kisses her on the cheek. Sylvia looks surprised for a moment and then puts out a hand to Amy's hair. Then she does another twirl

Amy moves to the desk and dials a number on the telephone

During the following, Sylvia finds the jigsaw box lid and looks at the picture as though she is looking at her reflection in a mirror. Amy does not see her

Amy (*into the phone*) Kate? It's Amy. ... Oh, not so bad. I was just wondering ... Well, I know it sounds silly, but I wondered if you have some clothes I could borrow tomorrow night. ... Something stylish, pretty, you know. ... Why? Well, I'm going out, you see. ... Yes. ... Well, I don't know exactly where but, well, I just want to look nice and I promised Trixie I wouldn't wear a cardigan. ... Colour? Oh, I hadn't thought. (*She turns and sees Sylvia looking at the lady in blue on the jigsaw lid*) Kate, have you got anything in blue?

CURTAIN

The same. Saturday evening, a month later

The window curtains are closed

When the CURTAIN *rises, Sylvia and Kate are sitting on the sofa. Kate is showing Sylvia a fashion magazine*

Kate Now, that I think is definitely cheap. Look, it does nothing for her at all, she's just falling out of it. I mean if you're going to wear a dress, you might as well wear it home again. Unless an obvious alternative arises of course. (*She turns over a page*) Oh, now, that's better. That's chic. You see the difference. Elegant and classy instead of brash and ridiculous. Of course, it helps to be able to wear it in a size 8. Oh look, do you like that? Now that would suit you, Sylvia. Not every one can wear red, but I think you could. Bring out a bit of colour in your cheeks.

During the following, Sylvia loses interest and fidgets with the corner of a cushion and the tassels on the sofa, then gets up and wanders over to the window

Except that no-one should be allowed to have legs that long. I bet she has real trouble getting trousers to fit. Serve her right too. (*She looks up at Sylvia*) What is it, Sylvia. Are you all right?
Sylvia What time is it?
Kate (*looking at her watch*) Just gone half-past nine. Are you tired? Do you want to go to bed?
Sylvia Amy's late.
Kate No she's not. She's rarely home before 10.30 on Saturdays. She's fine.
Sylvia It's a long day for her at school.
Kate (*realizing*) Oh yes. Well … (*She quickly looks at the magazine again*) Sylvia, do you think I should have my hair permed? I haven't had a perm for years. Do you know, my very first perm was a home perm that my mother did for me to give me curls for a Christmas party. It was supposed to make me look like Miss Pears of the Year. It turned out more like bubble monster of the decade. It was terrible. I cried for days.
Sylvia (*examining the curtain*) That isn't right.
Kate What isn't?
Sylvia I'm sure that isn't right. That shouldn't be there.
Kate What do you mean?
Sylvia This … this …
Kate Do you mean the curtain, Sylvia?

Sylvia Yes, this … It shouldn't be like that.

Kate Draw them back if you want to see out. Is that what you mean?

Sylvia What?

Kate (*getting up and going to the window*) Do you want me to do it? (*She draws back the curtains*)

Sylvia jumps, disorientated by the sudden sound and movement

Sylvia Oh!

Kate It's all right, Sylvia. Look, you can see out now.

Sylvia (*touching the window*) No, no. Not like that. It's … It's — all … (*Her hand shakes*) Where has it all gone?

Kate Where has what gone? What are you looking for?

Sylvia The … The blue.

Kate It's dark, Sylvia. Is that what you mean?

Sylvia The garden. All the sky. Little bits of blue …

Kate It's still there. You'll see it in the morning. It's just dark. That's why the curtains were drawn.

Sylvia looks at the curtains again and then moves away and wanders towards the stairs

Are you tired, Sylvia? Would you like to go to bed? I'll come up and sit with you if you like.

Sylvia stops and exits into the kitchen

What d'you want. Sylvia? Can I get you something? (*She moves towards the kitchen*)

The doorbell rings. Kate stops and looks uncertain as to what she should do

Listen, Sylvia, I'm just going to answer the door. Don't … Don't touch anything in there. I'll be right back.

Kate exits into the hall

(*Off*) Well, look who it is!

Colin (*off*) Hallo, there.

Kate (*off*) Won't you come in?

Colin and Kate enter. Colin is in his thirties and enjoys being debonair and charming

Kate (*calling*) Look Sylvia, here's Colin come to visit you. (*To Colin*) Do sit down. Sorry, Amy's not here at the moment.

Sylvia wanders back into the room

Colin Kate, isn't it?
Kate Yes. How clever of you to remember.
Colin Have you moved in or something?
Kate No, just visiting.
Colin It's just that every time I ring or call I seem to have you to reckon with.
Kate What do you mean, "every time you ring or call"? You rang once when I was here. That was six weeks ago. Do you mean you haven't telephoned or visited since?
Colin Six weeks? Is it as long as that?
Kate It is. And since Amy was out at the time, you presumably haven't spoken to her for a lot longer than that.
Colin No, as a matter of fact, I haven't. (*He raises his voice*) Hallo, Sylvia, how are you?
Kate She's not deaf.
Colin I know that. (*He gets up and goes to Sylvia and kisses her cheek*)

Sylvia looks puzzled

Kate It's Colin, Sylvia.
Sylvia (*her face breaking into a smile*) Colin. How lovely. Now where's Amy? She'll be so pleased to see you.
Kate Ecstatic.
Colin Yes, where is Amy?
Kate Out.
Colin Out?
Sylvia At school.
Colin What?
Kate Oh, do sit down, Colin. You know about Sylvia and Amy, surely.
Colin Oh, yes, of course. (*He sits*) Where is she really?
Kate Just out. Sylvia darling, would you like me to take you up to bed?
Sylvia But we have visitors.
Kate True. I'll get you a glass of milk. Want one, Colin?
Colin No thanks.
Kate Suit yourself.

Kate exits into the kitchen

Sylvia remains standing, staring at Colin

Colin Are you well, Aunt Sylvia?
Sylvia Quite well, thank you. Amy will be sorry to have missed you.

Colin Yes, I'm sorry to have missed her. Will she be late?
Sylvia Oh I hope not. I worry so if she's late from school. I should be going
to meet her. (*She moves towards the hall door*)

Kate enters with a glass of milk

(*Moving to retrieve Sylvia*) Come and sit down and drink your milk. Amy's
fine. It's not time to meet her yet.

Kate gets Sylvia to sit down and gives her the glass

(*Under her breath*) Thanks, Colin.
Colin Sorry. Just trying to ask after my cousin.
Kate She's out.
Colin So you said.
Kate And utterly unaccountable to you.
Colin Utterly. But your defensive need to protect her only makes me more
curious as to her whereabouts.
Kate I don't exactly know her whereabouts as she isn't accountable to me
either.
Colin But presumably she left the babysitter a contact number.
Kate What if she had?
Colin What is all this about, Kate?
Kate It's about you having a nerve. Amy doesn't hear from you or see you
for weeks at a time. Then you turn up out of the blue and imply that she's
neglecting Sylvia by going out for an evening.
Colin I'm implying no such thing. I'm just curious. What's the big secret?
Kate There is no secret. (*Pause*) If you must know, she's out with your
antiquarian bookseller, as she has been every Saturday evening for the last
month.
Colin (*after a pause*) Well, good for Gregory.
Kate It's good for Amy too.
Colin And so you're in charge here.
Kate I happen to be tonight. Trixie usually sits with Sylvia but she had a prior
engagement tonight. And as I just happened to be footloose and fancy free,
I volunteered. However, we think Amy may have to change her outings to
another night. Saturdays could cramp my style.
Colin I can believe that. So is it serious between Amy and Gregory?
Kate He makes her happy, I think. It's a strange thing, watching this slightly
old-fashioned courtship. He calls for her once a week and she borrows my
clothes and sparkles like a girl. Then she comes home and sheds her pretty
clothes and goes to bed alone.
Colin How quaint.

Kate It isn't really. Not when you see them together. Amy is …
Colin What?
Kate She's different, somehow. Alive. For the first time in years.
Colin Really smitten, eh?
Kate Quite possibly.
Colin He must be nearly twice her age.
Kate Don't be silly. There's ten years between them if that.
Colin More like fifteen. He's older than he looks.
Kate What does that matter? I think they're good for each other. Even if they do talk about books all the time.
Colin Amy always was one for books. How very typical of her. Not that it ever crossed my mind when I contacted Gregory about that find of hers. Well, well, how delightful.
Kate I'm not sure where it's going, however.
Colin Does it have to go anywhere?
Kate Presumably he won't still be calling for her once a week in another ten years.
Colin Stranger things have happened. And just because it wouldn't suit you doesn't mean it wouldn't suit Amy.
Kate She just may need to get a wider circle of babysitters, that's all.
Colin Was that a barbed comment?
Kate Possibly. Did it barb?
Colin I'm more than happy to spend an occasional evening with my aunt. Saturdays may not always be convenient however.
Kate What happened tonight? Were you stood up?
Colin No.
Kate What a shame.
Colin Were you?
Kate Certainly not.
Colin Well, there you are then. It's just that we both happened to be footloose and fancy free and destined to meet here together.
Sylvia Little bits of blue. Little bits of blue.
Kate You, me and Sylvia.
Sylvia It should be — blue.
Colin What's she mean?
Kate She's lost her sky, Colin.
Colin What?
Kate It's dark. She's lost the sky.
Colin Doesn't she understand about night and day any more?
Kate Not at this precise moment. Perhaps she'll remember tomorrow. Or at least be reassured.
Colin I didn't realize it had got this bad.
Kate Why should you? You haven't been here.

Colin I know, but …

There is the sound of the front door opening. Amy's and Gregory's voices are heard from the passage

Kate She's home.
Colin Oh. Amy's home, Aunt Sylvia.
Sylvia (*turning quickly at Colin's words*) Amy? Amy's home?
Kate Colin!
Colin Sorry, I didn't think.

Sylvia moves to the door and opens it

> *Amy and Gregory enter. Amy does look different but it is not just her clothes that have changed. There is a radiance about her and Gregory*

Sylvia (*looking past Colin and Amy into the hall*) Amy? Amy, are you there?

Sylvia exits into the hall, calling for Amy

Colin She's here, Aunt Sylvia.
Amy Colin? What are you doing here?
Colin Look, I'm sorry about all this. I didn't mean to confuse her.
Kate Good old Colin.
Amy Don't worry. She'll settle down in a moment.

Amy exits into the hall

(*Off*) Come on in, Sylvia. Everything's all right. Please come in.

Amy enters, leading a reluctant Sylvia

Sylvia But they said Amy was home.
Amy It was only me. I'm home. Everything's all right.
Sylvia They've taken the sky. That can't be right.
Amy What do you mean, darling? What's worrying you?
Kate She was disorientated by the dark and the drawn curtains. Look, it's getting late. And there are far too many people in this room as it is. I'll take her up to bed. You stay and talk to Colin.
Amy Oh, there's no need, Kate. I can do that.
Kate No, no. Make the most of him. He may have a relapse any time. Appendices can be funny things. I'll see to Sylvia.
Amy Are you sure? Is she all right?

Kate She will be. Come on, Sylvia. Will you come upstairs with me? You can help me draw the curtains in your room. And when you've had a sleep you'll see the sky again.

Amy Thank you, Kate. You're a dear. I'll come and see her in a moment.

Kate and Sylvia exit up the stairs

Amy watches them go upstairs

Colin I'm so sorry, Amy. I had no idea things had got this bad.

Amy It comes and goes, Colin. Some days are better than others. It's just that the bad days are getting a little more frequent.

Colin Does she really have no idea who you are?

Amy She knows I love her.

There is a pause. Gregory and Colin both look at Amy and then at each other

Colin (*trying to lighten things*) Hallo there, Gregory. Good to see you.

Gregory Yes, you too.

Colin So. Introducing you two proved — satisfactory.

Gregory Very. Thank you.

Colin Look, I just popped in to say hallo. I should have thought that it might not be convenient.

Gregory and Amy exchange a smile

(*Seeing the smile*) I won't hang around now. I really just wanted to make sure things were all right here.

Amy They're fine. Thank you, Colin. But it is good of you to come.

Colin Not at all. As Kate has reminded me, I probably don't come often enough. Are you really all right, Amy? I mean, if there is anything I could do you would let me know, wouldn't you? If things became more — difficult.

Amy We're fine. Really, Colin.

Colin Good. Well, I'll be going then. Good-night, all.

Amy Good-night, Colin. Thank you for calling. I'm sorry I wasn't in.

Colin Not at all. You deserve an evening out. Anyway, Kate entertained me royally. (*He moves to the door*)

Amy I bet she did. (*She follows him to the door*)

Colin Good-night, Gregory. Take care.

Gregory Yes. You too, Colin.

Amy and Colin exit into the hall

Gregory moves to the window, standing with his back to the door

Amy enters

Amy smiles and stands behind Gregory, putting her arms around him. He turns and embraces her

Amy I think that was a bit of a shock for Colin.
Gregory What was?
Amy You and me.
Gregory You mean, "What is she doing with an old codger like him?"
Amy Oh, no. Just surprised that you should look twice at a faded mouse like me. Colin doesn't associate me with men. I'm just little cousin Amy.
Gregory I could enlighten him on a few things then.
Amy Don't you dare.
Gregory I would simply tell him how wonderful you are and how much I love you.
Amy It sounds so strange. So unbelievable.
Gregory Why?
Amy Because I'm not used to such things. This has never happened to me before. And it's all happened so quickly. Why should I expect Colin to understand when I don't understand it myself?
Gregory Perhaps we're not meant to understand. Perhaps we're just meant to marvel. That's one of the joys of loving.
Amy Have you ever felt this before?
Gregory Once, longer ago than I really care to remember. I was in the throes of teenage love. It was agony.
Amy Why?
Gregory Because I never had the courage to tell her and she never noticed I was there.
Amy Poor Gregory.
Gregory I got over it.
Amy Did it take long?
Gregory Forever. Several weeks at least. And now you've come into my rather staid and lonely life and made it lovely. It was worth the wait. Now I can put a face to my dream. Someone to share it with. I have a dream of a house by the sea, with a library full of books and a desk by the window. And an attic bedroom where we could lie under the skylight and look up at the stars.
Amy Sounds wonderful.
Gregory It is.
Amy Colin probably thinks we talk about books all the time.
Gregory Well, we do talk about books.

Amy
Gregory } (*together*) Just not all the time.

They laugh and look at each other for a moment

Gregory There are so many things to talk about, Amy.

Amy So many dreams to catch up on?

Gregory It doesn't have to be a daydream. I don't mean the house and the skylight, but us. This is real. What we feel is so strong. Why can't we make real plans?

Amy (*turning away as though sensing danger*) You know, Colin used to say ——

Gregory Marry me, Amy?

Amy turns and looks at him and her longing to say "Yes" is clearly visible in her face. Then she turns slowly away

Amy I can't.

Gregory Why not?

Amy (*looking towards the stairs*) Because I'm needed here.

Gregory You're needed here, too.

Amy I know. And I need you. And I long for us to be together. Believe me. I have never longed for anything more in my life. But I can't leave her. I'm all she has.

Gregory Dearest Amy, she doesn't even know who you are any more.

Amy I can't be sure of that. I still represent something for her. Stability. Calm. And besides, I know who I am. I know what I meant to her, what she did for me all her life. Now it's my turn.

Gregory But does it have to be you?

Amy You haven't seen her when she is at her most frightened and distressed. I'm at least a familiar face to her in that very dark storm. I can still help her find her way.

Gregory But there are places ...

Amy No. I couldn't. I couldn't send her away. She's lost anywhere but here. This is her home. I'm her family. I can't abandon her. Please don't ask me to do that.

Gregory All right. I won't. I'm sorry.

Amy Besides, we still have each other, don't we. We're not saying goodbye, are we?

Gregory Of course not. Of course we still have each other.

Amy Am I doing a very selfish thing? I ought to say find someone else, Gregory, someone who can people your dream for you. But I don't think I'm that brave. Is that very selfish of me?

Gregory No, it's not selfish. Besides, no other face would fit.

Amy I realized some time ago that life was going to be different for me. And I thought, this is it now. It's not as I once imagined but this is it now. I knew that I couldn't leave but I would think, what if ... Then I met you, and it's as if I've found a part of myself. I couldn't bear to be without you now.

Gregory Nor could you bear to leave her? Is that it?

Amy Yes. That's it. But thank you, Gregory. Thank you for asking me. I'll always remember that you asked me. I'll have that to treasure. (*She reaches up and kisses him passionately*)

Kate enters down the stairs. She sees Amy and Gregory and smiles, then continues down the stairs, unaware of the anguish they are feeling

Kate Colin gone then?

Amy and Gregory break away from each other

Obviously. Silly question, Kate. Still, he might have offered to see a girl home.

Gregory Can I take you?

Kate Oh no, thank you. I have the transport. It was just the company I was after, and I think you're already spoken for. (*She winks at him*) Well, goodnight, children. I'll see myself out.

Amy Thanks for coming, Kate. You know how much I appreciate it.

Kate I most certainly do. (*She blows Amy a kiss*)

Kate exits into the hall

Amy She's a dear, isn't she?

Gregory Yes.

Amy So are you.

Gregory Thank you.

Amy Don't feel rejected, please. It isn't you.

Gregory I know. I don't feel rejected. I know that you would have said yes, if you possibly could. I just feel sad. Because I believe that we were meant to be together.

Amy We are. You don't have to go just yet, do you?

Gregory No, not just yet.

Amy Will you do something for me?

Gregory Anything.

Amy Dance with me?

Gregory What?

Amy I've never danced with anyone.

Gregory I don't know how.

Amy moves to the CD player and selects some music

Oh, I don't mean proper dancing. I don't know how to, either. I just mean — dance with me. You know.
Gregory Wherever the music takes us?
Amy That's right. (*She switches on the CD player*)

The CD plays: we hear the Everly Brothers singing "Let It Be Me"

Gregory Is this yours? You must be older than I thought.
Amy I'm a girl of very catholic tastes.
Gregory Walter Scott and the Everly Brothers. What a team?
Amy (*moving to stand by Gregory*) Dance with me?

Gregory takes Amy in his arms and they move gently together to the music for a minute or two

Sylvia enters down the stairs

Gregory and Amy do not see Sylvia. She stands and watches them. Then Gregory sees Sylvia over Amy's shoulder

Gregory Sylvia?
Amy (*turning round, startled*) Aunt Sylvia, I thought you were asleep. Are you all right?
Sylvia I mustn't sleep. Didn't you know that? I have to wait. I always wait up for her when she's out.

Sylvia moves to the window and looks out

Sylvia Where's Amy?
Amy (*wearily, full of emotion*) I don't know.
Sylvia I miss her when she's away.
Amy (*looking at Sylvia with great tenderness*) She misses you too.
Sylvia When will she be back?

Amy moves behind Sylvia and puts her arms around her, mirroring the way she embraced Gregory earlier. Gregory watches them

Amy Would I do, just this once, until she comes home?

Sylvia does not reply but continues to look out of the window. Gregory watches Amy, moved by her gentleness

CURTAIN

ACT II
Scene 1

A Saturday afternoon, several weeks later

A "Happy Birthday" banner decorates the back wall and there several hooks on the walls. A bag of balloons and several inflated balloons tied together with string are on the desk, along with Ivanhoe. *There is a newspaper on the coffee table and a pile of plates and paper napkins on the sideboard*

When the Curtain *rises, Amy is vacuuming and Sylvia is wandering around the room, obviously agitated by the noise of the vacuum cleaner. Sylvia keeps getting in Amy's way; Amy gently moves her aside and continues vacuuming, always with one eye on Sylvia. Then she turns off the vacuum cleaner*

Amy All finished, Aunt Sylvia. I'm sorry about the noise, but I'd put it off too long. The place was a disgrace, and you wanted it to look nice for the party, didn't you? Sit down now. No more noise, I promise. It's all right.

Amy exits into the kitchen with the vacuum cleaner

(*Off*) You've still not finished this lunch. What am I going to do with you? You'll fade away.

Amy enters from the kitchen

Will you make up for it later? Eat lots of tea? It's a special occasion, remember? (*She tidies up the newspaper and put them on the desk, then picks up* Ivanhoe *and smiles*) Good old Walter Scott. (*She turns to Sylvia*) Could you put that back in the bookshelf for me, Aunt Sylvia?

Sylvia comes hesitantly towards Amy and takes the book from her hand

Could you put it on the shelf? Over there? (*She points to the bookshelf*) Put it with the others over there.

Sylvia looks puzzled and looks at the book again. She sits down on the sofa. She opens the book and finds that the pages are still uncut. She tries to turn them. Amy sits down beside her

Amy That was the book that Gregory came to look at. Do you remember?
I thought it might be valuable because the pages weren't cut. But it wasn't.
So I just have a book with uncut pages. Quite a novelty. I'll get round to
cutting them soon. Then I'll read it. Do you remember the story? *Ivanhoe*?
Sylvia (*still fiddling with the book*) No.
Amy Never mind. (*She gets up and continues to tidy the room*)
Sylvia This isn't right.
Amy I'll get round to it soon.
Sylvia All wrong. (*She tears the join in one of the uncut pages*)
Amy Oh no, don't do that. You'll spoil it. I'll do it later. (*She moves quickly
to the sofa and takes hold of the book*)

Sylvia hangs on

Let me have it, please!

A page rips

LET GO!

*Sylvia is startled by Amy's voice. She lets the book go and huddles on the sofa,
clutching a cushion. Amy is also startled by her own anger. She tries to
smooth down the torn pages, then closes the book very gently and puts it on
the bookshelf. She turns back to Sylvia*

(*Too calmly*) I'm sorry, Aunt Sylvia. I didn't mean to shout. It's just that
I didn't want the book spoiled. It … It means a lot to me. That's all. I'm
sorry. (*She moves to the desk, visibly trying to calm herself. Then she picks
up the bag of balloons and moves back to the sofa*) Would you like to help
me blow the balloons up? Have you got lots of puff?

*Amy blows up a balloon. Sylvia gradually realizes what is happening and
watches with interest and laughs*

Sylvia How pretty.
Amy Yes. You try. (*She finds a blue balloon*) Look, here's a blue one. Blue's
your colour.
Sylvia No. No. Red. Red is my colour. Kate said so.
Amy Did she? Well, Kate should know. Have a red one then.

*Amy blows up the blue balloon. Sylvia looks at the balloons, puzzled again,
picking up one at a time. Amy selects a red one and gives it to her*

Amy Red.
Sylvia Red?
Amy That's right. (*She leans forward and kisses Sylvia*)
Sylvia Red.
Amy Blue, red. All we need is white. Then it will be a patriotic party.

Sylvia does not respond

You're right. Who wants patriotism. It's a birthday. Let's go for green —
and purple. Let's go really mad.

*Amy blows up a few more balloons. Sylvia also has a go but cannot tie the
knots. They laugh. Amy tosses the balloons around the room*

Oh, the times we've done this, you and me. Only it used to be me who
couldn't tie the knots.

Pause

(*Turning to Sylvia*) Aunt Sylvia, do you know what day it is today?
Sylvia Day?
Amy Yes. What day is it?
Sylvia (*searching for a familiar word*) Um it's … Oh … You know. That
day. Tuesday.
Amy That's not what I meant. Never mind. Don't worry.

Sylvia wanders around the room again, then exits into the kitchen

There is the sound of a key in the lock and the front door opening and closing

*Gregory enters carrying a bottle of champagne in a gift bag. He puts it on
the sideboard*

Amy runs to Gregory and they embrace

Gregory (*holding up a Yale key*) I used it. Do you mind?
Amy Of course not. That's why I gave it to you.
Gregory Happy birthday, my love!
Amy Thank you, Gregory.

Amy and Gregory kiss

Sylvia wanders back into the living-room

Gregory breaks away from Amy

Gregory How is she?
Amy Ask her.
Gregory Hallo, Sylvia. How are you today?
Sylvia Today? It's not Tuesday?
Gregory No. It's Saturday.
Amy Never mind.

The doorbell rings

Excuse me.

Amy exits into the hall

Sylvia Saturday. Is it Saturday?
Gregory Yes. It's Am ... We're going to have a party. Remember?
Sylvia That's right. Of course. We've been — getting ready.
Gregory So I see. Well done.

Amy and Colin enter

Colin Hallo, Gregory. Hallo, Aunt Sylvia. And happy birthday, little cousin.
Another year older. (*He kisses Amy*)
Amy Thank you, Colin.

Colin looks from Gregory to Amy and then makes up his mind

Colin Now I have a suggestion to make. Why don't I let you two get ready
for this — occasion, while I take my beautiful aunt out for a spin.
Amy What?
Colin (*lowering his voice slightly*) Come on. I'm not daft. It's probably the
only time you two will have alone together today.
Amy It's very kind, Colin, but it's a while since she's been out. She may not
be happy ...
Colin Nonsense. (*He moves to Sylvia and slips her arm through his*) Sylvia
is just dying to come out with me, aren't you?
Sylvia With you?
Colin Heard about me, eh? Well, you can't believe everything you hear!
What do you say? You would do me a great honour.
Sylvia (*laughing*) I remember you. Always were a ... a ...
Colin Precisely.
Amy You'd better let me take her to the bathroom first.
Colin Oh, we won't be that long. Just a little drive. We'll be back before you
know it.

Colin escorts Sylvia to the door, then turns back with a wink

So make the most of it.

Colin and Sylvia exit

Gregory turns to Amy and holds out his arms. She moves to him and they embrace

Gregory Happy birthday.
Amy You've said that already.
Gregory I know. I just wanted to say it again. And to remind you how much I love you.
Amy I know you do. I never have any doubts about that.
Gregory Should I stop saying it then?
Amy No. Never stop saying it.
Gregory All right. I won't.
Amy (*moving away*) Come on. We can't stand around like this. We've got work to do. (*During the following, she stands on a chair and fixes some balloons to the hooks on the wall*)
Gregory Balloons?
Amy Balloons. Food. Candles. We have guests arriving.

Gregory stands at the door to the kitchen and looks in

Gregory Yes, so I see. Quite a spread.
Amy All old favourites.

Gregory exits into the kitchen

Gregory (*off*) Iced gems and jam sandwiches? Are these really your favourites?
Amy They used to be once. Isn't it disgusting?
Gregory (*off*) Which birthday did you say it was?
Amy You know perfectly well.
Gregory (*off*) Aha! I've found the candles.
Amy There won't be enough.
Gregory (*off*) Where shall I put them?
Amy Haven't you found the *pièce de resistance*?
Gregory (*off*) You mean the chocolate cake?
Amy Of course. Amy's favourite.

Gregory enters and lifts Amy down from the chair

Gregory Do you know what I had planned? Cold chicken, French bread and champagne. And a large red rug spread under a chestnut tree. And you could lie down and look at the sky while I dropped grapes in your mouth.

Amy (*laughing*) How do you know I'd rather do that than have balloons and iced gems?

Gregory Because you're more grown-up than you used to be.

They laugh. Gregory pulls Amy close to kiss her

Amy Well, we can still do that another time.

Gregory I wanted it to be on your birthday.

Amy But I've always spent my birthday with Aunt Sylvia.

Gregory Then perhaps it's about time for a change.

Amy, suddenly subdued, disengages herself from Gregory and moves away to fix more balloons

Amy We'll go another day, Gregory.

Gregory (*sighing*) Amy, this is all very — well — touching, even quaint, but is it … I mean — is it healthy?

Amy What do you mean?

Gregory Who is all this for?

Amy For Amy.

Gregory puts his hands on Amy's shoulders. For a moment he seems to want to shake her but when he speaks it is with great gentleness

Gregory My dearest girl, you *are* Amy. There is no other. Is this really what you want?

Amy All right then. It's for Aunt Sylvia.

Gregory Aunt Sylvia? Does she even know what day it is?

Amy (*defiantly*) Yes. Yes, somewhere inside her she does know. Doing this … Well — it might help. To remind her.

Gregory But it isn't fair. You're trying to remind her of something that no longer exists. Amy has grown up. She's a woman, not a child.

Amy You're doing it too.

Gregory What?

Amy Talking about Amy in the third person. It's catching, isn't it?

Gregory (*after a pause*) I'd call it sinister.

Amy looks at Gregory for a moment and moves away, disturbed

Amy How strange.

Gregory What is?

Amy That you should use that word.

Gregory That's how it feels.

Amy And you haven't lived with it the way I have. Do you know, there have been times when I've played the game too well. It's like living with a ghost in the house, the ghost of my former self living with me day by day. Sometimes I even think I hear her. I become expectant, almost as expectant as Sylvia. I wait for Amy to come home from school. I worry about her when she is late and I bake chocolate cakes for her tea.

Gregory Amy, don't. Can't you see what's happening to you? It's such a waste. You have a life to live. You shouldn't be shutting yourself away in some lost childhood to appease a woman who doesn't even remember who you are.

Amy I'm trying to help her remember.

Gregory No, my love, you are not. You are allowing her to believe something that is no longer true. It's becoming a prison for you both. You should be helping her to look forward.

Amy Don't you understand? Aunt Sylvia can't look forward.

Gregory So instead you help her look back.

Amy Yes, in a way. Because soon she won't even be able to do that. All her memories are being lost, one by one. Can you imagine how lonely that must be? I'm trying to give her something, some safe place where she can still feel — alive.

Gregory It's impossible, Amy. Impossible. You'll only end up locking both her and yourself into the past. You'll die there. Believe me, you'll die. Get out now. Before it's too late.

Amy I can't.

Gregory I'm not saying it for my sake, Amy. I'm saying it for yours. Even if you don't want to marry me, just try to stop all this — pretending.

Amy I do want to marry you.

Gregory Yet you won't.

Amy I've told you. I can't.

Gregory What about your future? One day it will be you looking back. Won't you regret it?

Amy Regret not abandoning her?

Gregory Regret abandoning a future, a life, your own self. Do you really know who you are any more? You have to be true to yourself.

Amy But at what cost? I'd have to hurt the one person who has loved me all my life. She doesn't deserve that.

Gregory Why would you hurt her?

Amy I wouldn't be with her any more.

Gregory You could visit her. It's not as if you'd never see her again.

Amy She needs to be here. This is her home. She needs me. Without me she'd be lost, and totally alone. Because I share her memories. I hold them for her. She'd be lost in a no man's land, always waiting.
Gregory She's waiting now.
Amy What?
Gregory She waits for Amy. And Amy never comes home from school, does she? Never.

They look at each other for a long moment. Amy is shaken

The doorbell rings

  Amy exits into the hall

Gregory sighs and takes a swipe at the balloons

Trixie (*off*) Hallo, hallo. Happy birthday, Amy.
Amy Thank you, Trixie. Come in. Hallo, Kate.

  Trixie, Kate and Amy enter. Trixie is carrying bags of shopping; she and Kate both carry birthday presents

Trixie Contributions and rations and gin. Where shall I put them?
Amy (*indicating the kitchen*) Bring them in here, Trixie.

  Trixie and Amy exit into the kitchen

Kate looks around the room, then goes to Gregory and puts a hand on his shoulder

Kate So, where are all the kiddywinks?
Gregory All grown up, I think, Kate.
Kate Eerie, isn't it?
Gregory And infinitely sad.
Kate Yes, you don't exactly look in party mood, Gregory. Not had a lovers' tiff have you?
Gregory (*sighing*) No.

  Amy and Trixie enter from the kitchen

Kate Well, birthday girl, how are you? (*She gives the present to Amy*)
Amy Fine, thank you, Kate. Thank you for coming.

Kate (*sitting down on the sofa*) You're welcome. Just make sure I win "Pass the Parcel".

Amy is uncomfortable and looks at Gregory. Kate notices the look. Amy moves away and puts Kate's present on the desk

Kate Don't worry, Gregory. We don't really go through with this charade, you know. Except for the decorations and eats. If we're very good, we're allowed a grown-up drink at the end to toast the health of the birthday girl.

Amy Kate.

Kate You haven't forgotten the grown-up drinks have you, Amy?

Trixie If she has, I know where there's a secret supply of gin. And I've just topped it up. Let me look at you, Amy. You're tired, dear. How are things?

Amy Fine.

Trixie Where's Sylvia?

Amy Colin's taken her out for a drive while we got ready. She was worrying about — everything.

Kate Who invited Colin?

Amy I did. He always used to come to my … (*She catches Gregory's eye and moves to sit by Kate*) Anyway, he'll be back soon.

Kate Don't get me wrong, Amy, I'll be delighted to see him. It was just a surprise, that's all. Good job I put my best underwear on, isn't it?

Amy Why? What's your underwear got to do with it?

Kate You've come on leaps and bounds, Amy, but you could still learn a good deal. A girl must always be prepared. It makes her feel — prepared. (*She whispers to Amy, then adds*) And wait until you see what I've given you for your birthday!

Amy (*laughing*) Kate! Is it safe to open in public? (*She glances at the present on the desk*)

Kate That depends on your public. I'm starving. Can we start on the nibbles?

Amy Yes, help yourself.

Kate Help myself? What sort of party is this?

Amy Mine. I'm the birthday girl.

Kate (*suddenly serious*) You are tired, aren't you?

Amy I'm fine, Kate. (*Cheerfully*) Go and get the sausages.

Kate (*rising and heading for the kitchen*) If you want something doing, do it yourself.

Kate exits into the kitchen

Trixie (*following Kate to the door but not into the kitchen*) Oh, check the oven, will you, Kate? I've put some pizza in.

Gregory moves to the back of the sofa, leans down and kisses the top of Amy's head. Trixie turns in time to see this and smiles. She moves towards them

Trixie I can't tell you how much good it does me to see you two. You know, you ought to get away and spend some proper time together.
Amy A lovely idea, Trixie, but not very practical.

Amy exits into the kitchen

Trixie Timing never was my strong point. Sorry. Is there a problem?
Gregory Conflict of loyalties, that's all.
Trixie Be gentle with her. It's not easy.
Gregory I can see that.
Trixie She's been doing a marvellous job for a long time. Until fairly recently she wouldn't go out at all. It was difficult to persuade her to let anyone else look after Sylvia. Kate and I are the privileged few. But you're something else. You've given her something — how shall I put it — a sparkle.
Gregory I'd like to give her a future. A life.
Trixie I believe you would. And I can see what she gives you too. That shouldn't be allowed to fade.
Gregory I can't put any pressure on her. She needs to want to be with me.
Trixie Oh, she wants you. Have no doubt about that. But that is often when it's the most difficult. When what we want is just out of reach.
Gregory This is within reach if only she'd see it.
Trixie She views it differently. Near and yet impossibly far. Because Sylvia is more than a duty or an obligation, you see. She was once Amy's whole life. It's difficult for her to move on.
Gregory Difficult, yes. Change is often difficult. But it shouldn't be impossible. Surely there comes a time when we have to move on. For her sake. For sanity's sake.
Trixie Surely you exaggerate?
Gregory No, Trixie, I don't think I do. This can't go on. I believe she'll break.
Trixie (*patting Gregory's arm*) Amy is stronger than we sometimes give her credit for.

The noise of Colin's and Sylvia's return comes from the hall

Colin (*off*) It's all right. You're home. You're quite safe.
Sylvia Amy! Amy! Amy!

Amy and Kate enter quickly from the kitchen. Kate is carrying a plate of sausages which she puts on the sideboard

Colin and Sylvia enter from the hall. Colin is very flustered, Sylvia disorientated and distressed

Colin I don't know what happened. Some sort of panic attack. She tried to get out of the car.
Sylvia Everywhere. Everywhere. All over … All over … Amy! Amy!
Amy It's all right, Aunt Sylvia. You're safe here. It's all right.

Amy leads Sylvia to an armchair

Trixie What frightened her? What happened?
Colin I don't know. She just got more and more agitated. Pulling at the seat belt, pulling at me. Then she went for the car door. I really thought we were going to have an accident. There was nothing I could do except pray and head back here.
Trixie Didn't you stop?
Colin I'd never have got her back in the car.
Amy What frightened you? Can you tell me?
Sylvia (*gesturing with her hands*) Everywhere. Couldn't … Couldn't … Everywhere. All so … (*She rocks backwards and forwards, very distressed*)
Amy It's a long time since she's been out in a car.
Kate Could it have been that? The traffic? The noise?
Colin I suppose so, but I've never seen anyone react like that. It was crazy.
Amy She's not crazy, Colin. She just lost her bearings. She can't make sense of things any more.
Colin I thought she was going to kill us both.
Kate Perhaps she thought the same thing of you.
Amy (*kneeling by Sylvia's chair*) It's all right, darling. You're quite safe here. Look. You see? You're home. You know this place. You know me. Look. Everything is all right.

Sylvia becomes quieter but continues to rock slightly. She looks around the room. She sees the balloons and points at them with a shaking hand

Sylvia What …? What … ?
Amy Balloons. For a party. Do you remember? They won't hurt you. We've decorated the room. For a party. It's Amy's birthday.
Sylvia Amy's?
Amy Yes, that's right.
Trixie I'm so glad you're here, Sylvia. I need you to help me put the candles on the cake.
Colin Just don't let her light them.
Gregory Steady, Colin.
Colin I need a drink.
Kate Trixie, tell him where the gin is. Put him out of his misery.
Trixie In the kitchen, second cupboard on the right. Pour one for Sylvia too.
Amy I'm not sure that's very wise.

Trixie Nonsense. She's been terrified. If Colin can have one, so can Sylvia. It's her gin. She can probably hold it better than he can.

Colin What's that supposed to mean?

Kate It means it's only five o'clock in the afternoon.

Colin It's Saturday.

Kate Oh. Do you usually attack the gin on Saturday afternoons?

Colin Only when I've been out with …

Kate (*glaring at him*) With your aunt.

Colin Honestly, Kate, it was …

Kate takes Colin's hand and leads him towards the kitchen

Kate Oh, poor Colin. Come and tell Kate all about it.

Colin and Kate exit into the kitchen

Colin (*off*) You've no idea …

Gregory Is there anything I can do? Should we call the doctor?

Amy I don't think so. She was just frightened.

Sylvia Amy … Amy …

Amy You're safe, Aunt Sylvia. Nothing can hurt you. You're safe.

Trixie (*rubbing Sylvia's hands*) Her hands are so cold. (*She continues to rub Sylvia's hands during the following*)

Gregory It's probably the shock. She really is in a state. Shouldn't we call the doctor, Amy?

Amy I don't think so. It would just frighten her more. She'll calm down soon. Won't you, Aunt Sylvia? You'll be fine, won't you, once you've remembered where you are. You'll know that there's nothing to be frightened of.

Sylvia (*looking at Trixie's hands which are still rubbing her own*) Her hands. Her poor hands.

Trixie I'm trying to warm them, Sylvia.

Sylvia All in bits. Did you know that? All in bits. Her poor hands.

Kate enters from the kitchen carrying a tray of drinks including a glass of gin and tonic for Sylvia. Colin follows with sandwiches and biscuits. They put the drinks and food on the sideboard

Kate Here you are, this will warm you up, Sylvia.

Amy Are you sure this is a good idea?

Trixie Of course.

Kate (*giving Sylvia a glass of gin and tonic*) There you are, Sylvia. We couldn't wait, so we'll have it now. It will make you feel better.

Amy Not on an empty stomach, it won't.

Kate Best way to take it, if you ask me.
Trixie Amy has a point. Colin, get something for Sylvia to eat, would you?
Gregory I'll get it. Sandwich be all right?
Trixie Anything.

*Gregory puts a couple of sandwiches and a sausage on a plate. Kate hands
Colin a glass*

Kate Drink up, Colin.
Gregory (*holding the plate out to Sylvia*) Here you are, Sylvia. Try a little
of this.

Sylvia shakes her head and pushes the plate away

Amy Please?
Gregory Just a little?

*Sylvia rocks again, wringing her hands. During the following, Gregory
continues to try to coax Sylvia to eat. Sylvia sits still but her hands are
constantly on the move*

Amy We're crowding her. That never helps.
Trixie Look, let's just relax and get on with the party. Then perhaps Sylvia
will feel able to join in. Let's just make everything as normal as possible.
(*She breaks away; during the following she picks up plates of food and
offers it around*) Come on everyone, sit down, have something to eat. Then
we'll light the candles.
Amy Yes, that's a good idea. (*She gets up from her knees and goes to help
Trixie*)
Trixie I'd suggest putting the kettle on, but personally I think tea is over-
rated.
Colin (*sitting on the sofa*) Absolutely.
Kate (*sitting beside Colin*) Then be an angel and get me another drink.
Colin Finished already?
Kate I was thirsty.
Colin I think you'd better tuck in or you'll get squiffy.

Colin takes Kate's glass, gets up and exits into the kitchen

Kate What a wonderful word that is. Squiffy. Almost worth getting there just
to see if you can still say it.
Trixie No need. If I know you, Kate, you could be under the table and still
be able to recite the Greek alphabet.

Kate That's incredible. Because I can't recite the Greek alphabet when I'm not squiffy.

Colin enters from the kitchen with Kate's glass. He gives the glass to Kate and sits on the sofa beside her

Colin What will it be then, sausage or iced gems?
Kate No smoked salmon?
Amy Here you are, both of you. (*She offers them some food*)
Kate No smoked salmon. But I'd just like you to know, Amy, that this is the best party I've been to since … since … Well, since your last party.
Amy (*quietly*) Thank you, Kate.
Kate You're welcome.

Trixie exits into the kitchen

Amy moves back to Sylvia's chair where Gregory is still trying to coax Sylvia to eat

Amy How are you getting on?
Gregory Not brilliantly.
Amy She doesn't eat enough to keep a bird alive anyway. She'll forget how, one of these days.

Trixie enters from the kitchen with a chocolate cake with candles on it and a box of matches and a cake knife. She puts these items down on the coffee table

Trixie Here we are.
Kate Oh, cake already? In my day you had to eat all the sandwiches first.
Colin And then it was jelly.
Kate Green jelly.
Colin In the shape of a rabbit.
Kate I didn't know you were at that party. Which one were you?
Colin The cute one with the bow tie.
Kate Little dear.
Trixie Come on now, Gregory. You light the candles, and then Amy can blow them out and cut the cake.
Kate Just like a wedding, isn't it?
Trixie Steady, Kate. (*She moves round to the table and picks up the matches*)
Kate Sorry.
Gregory Here we go. (*He takes the matches from Kate, lights the candles, then puts the box down*)
Amy I told you you'd never find enough.

Sylvia Oh look at the pretty … pretty — whatsits.
Kate (*to Sylvia*) Candles.
Trixie Are you ready everyone? Sylvia, dear, are you ready to sing "Happy Birthday"?
Sylvia That isn't right.
Trixie Yes it is. Altogether now!

Trixie, Kate, Colin and Gregory all sing "Happy Birthday" to Amy. During the song Sylvia stands and comes forward to look at the cake

Sylvia No, no. That's not right. I know it's not right.
Colin All right, so there aren't enough candles, Aunt Sylvia. But who's counting? (*He turns to Amy*) Come on, little cousin. Blow them all out.
Sylvia (*increasingly agitated*) No, you mustn't. We must wait for her.

Amy blows out the candles

Trixie What is it, Sylvia?
Sylvia (*angrily*) You've blown out her candles. You've blown out Amy's candles.

Amy looks startled. Gregory puts his arm around Amy

Sylvia How could you do this? How could you?
Colin Oh, please God, no.
Gregory This has gone far enough.
Sylvia Where's Amy? I want Amy. I want Amy. What have you done with her? Where is she? Amy! Amy!
Amy Aunt Sylvia!
Trixie (*to Amy*) It's all right. She doesn't know what she's saying.
Gregory On the contrary, she's probably the only one of us who does know what she's saying.
Amy Gregory.
Colin Not now, Gregory. It's not the time.

Sylvia sees the box of matches and picks them up

Sylvia We'll have to do it again, when Amy comes home.
Amy No, Aunt Sylvia. Not the matches. Give them to me. Please. (*She moves quickly to Sylvia and makes to take the matches from her*)
Sylvia No. No. I shall keep them. I'll light them. For Amy.
Amy (*sternly*) Let me have them, Aunt Sylvia.
Sylvia (*frantic to hold on to the matches as though to some lifeline*) No, no, no!

Gregory Amy, be careful.
Amy (*grabbing hold of Sylvia's arm; also becoming frantic*) Let me have
them.

*Sylvia, very frightened, cries but will not let go of the matches. Amy, fearing
for her aunt's safety and visibly upset, tightens her grip*

Sylvia Ooh!
Amy Give them to me!
Trixie Amy, dear!
Amy Give them to me now!

*Sylvia suddenly raises her free arm and strikes Amy in the face. Amy reels
back. Gregory tries to take her in his arms, but she is too shocked to respond*

Colin (*moving to Sylvia's other side*) Be an angel and give me the matches,
Sylvia. I promise not to light the candles again without asking you.

*Sylvia, shocked and frightened herself, suddenly becomes limp and drops the
box of matches. Colin retrieves them and puts them in his pocket, then gently
guides Sylvia back to her armchair*

Thank you, Sylvia. Now, come and sit down.
Gregory Amy, you've got to get away from here.
Sylvia Is the lady all right?

*There is a pause. Colin looks across at Amy, surprised at the reference to "the
lady". Then he looks back at Sylvia*

Colin Yes, I think so.
Sylvia Did I hurt her?

There is a pause. Sylvia looks around at all the faces. No-one answers

(*To Amy*) Did I hurt you, dear?
Amy (*almost whispering*) It was nothing.

*Sylvia holds out a hand to Amy. Amy, after a moment's hesitation, slowly
crosses to Sylvia's chair and kneels down beside her. Sylvia puts her hand
on Amy's cheek*

Sylvia I didn't mean to hurt you. I'm sorry.
Amy I'm sorry too.

Sylvia You're a good kind girl. I didn't mean to hurt you. It's such a sweet
face. And it bothers me, because ... You see — the silly thing is — I can't
for the life of me remember who you are.

*There is a long pause. Everyone stares at Sylvia and Amy. Then, very slowly,
Amy rises to her feet, turns away from Sylvia and moves towards the stairs.
She moves as though in her sleep, hurt and shocked*

Should I know you? It's very silly of me. (*Pause*) Would someone please
tell me the young lady's name?

Amy reaches the bottom of the stairs and turns to face Sylvia

Amy (*very quietly*) There's nothing to tell.

Curtain

Scene 2

The same. A few minutes later

The party food is cleared away except for the cake

When the Curtain *rises Sylvia is asleep in the armchair. Kate is on the sofa
with a drink. Colin is standing behind the sofa with his hands in his pockets*

Trixie enters from the kitchen

Trixie I suppose most of it will keep, but I don't know who's going to eat
it.
Kate Make a doggy-bag up for Colin.
Colin No, thanks.
Trixie Do you think she's all right?
Colin Well, she wasn't showing many signs of being all right when she left
us.
Kate Not the best birthday a girl ever had.
Colin A fiasco from start to finish.
Kate It never used to be. Somehow we got through it all. It even used to be
fun.
Trixie Things have happened in the last year, haven't they? To Amy, I mean.
Kate You mean, Gregory has happened to Amy.
Trixie Yes. It's difficult pretending to be one thing in one world when you've
discovered yourself in another.

Kate Amy's in love. She should be allowed all the privileges and freedoms of being in love.

Trixie Privileges don't come without responsibilities.

Kate Fiddle faddle. Amy has had a life full of responsibility.

Gregory enters down the stairs

Trixie How is she?

Gregory She's locked her door. I can't get her to answer me.

Trixie She's had a big shock. Give her time.

Gregory Do you still think that I don't give her strength enough credit, Trixie? I knew it would break her.

Kate She hasn't broken yet, you know.

Trixie No, she hasn't. She's grieving.

Gregory She's heartbroken. And the worst of it is, I watched it happen. I feel I'm to blame.

Colin Nonsense. This isn't your fault.

Gregory My loving her has caused a conflict. If I hadn't asked her to marry me …

Trixie Colin's absolutely right. This isn't your fault. Your love has given Amy something wonderful. It's helped her through difficult times. There were signs of tension long before you came on the scene.

Gregory I wish I could believe you.

Trixie Believe me. There were. I saw them.

Gregory But you told me that Amy was strong.

Trixie She is. And she'll get through this. And that's the important thing. Not trying to decide who's to blame.

Kate Life is to blame. It's a sod sometimes.

Gregory So what's going to happen now?

Colin Well, it can't go on as it was, that's for sure. Something fundamental shifted here this afternoon. Some connection has been broken.

Gregory I think it broke some time ago. It's just that Amy couldn't bring herself to see it.

Colin Yes, you're probably right. But now she does know.

Gregory Yes. The make-believe is over.

Colin I presume that's what you meant when you said that Sylvia was the only one who knew what she was saying.

Gregory I just felt suddenly that she was the only one not pretending. She at least believed herself. The rest of us knew that we were playing some bizarre game, and trying to convince Sylvia that it was true. We could be accused of neglect. If not abuse.

Trixie Amy never meant it like that.

Gregory Of course she didn't. All I'm saying is that in her concern and love for Sylvia she's made promises that she can never keep. She tried to build her a refuge based on lies. It was doomed to failure. For both of them. And despite the fact that I would lie down and die for her, I had to stand by and watch it happen.

Kate Like I said. Life is a sod sometimes.

Gregory It shouldn't have been, Kate. With the way we feel about each other it could have been so good.

Kate It still can be. Take her away. Give her a life. The sort of life most only dream about.

Gregory I tried to. She couldn't come. Perhaps I should have suggested we stayed here and looked after Sylvia together.

Colin You couldn't have done that. It would have been no life at all, and certainly no start to a marriage. You'd have been sucked into the make-believe with them and drowned in it. It would have driven you all crazy.

Gregory At least I would have been here to support her.

Colin You were here today when it all fell apart.

Gregory To what end?

Trixie Loving Amy, of course. What other end is there?

Kate And she loves you. Like mad. Oh, this is not what I had in mind for the day, at all. She hasn't even opened her birthday present. What a waste.

Gregory (*moving to the back of Sylvia's chair and looking down at her*) And what about the other love of Amy's life? What's going to happen to her?

Colin Frankly I can't see them coping here on their own. Not after this.

Gregory Neither can I.

Colin Amy and I need to talk. After all, I'm her nearest relative.

Kate Don't tell me you're going to look after Sylvia?

Colin Well, if it means giving up my job and becoming a full-time carer, then, quite frankly, no, I can't see myself doing it. One little trip out in the car showed me that. But I suppose I have to take some sort of responsibility.

Kate I'm seeing an unsuspected side of the boy.

Trixie Amy always said that Colin would be here if she needed him.

Colin Did she?

Kate Yes, she did. She just never believed she would need you.

Colin I have to say that I never relished the thought of being needed. I suppose I did my fair share of believing what I wanted to believe.

Kate Oh, we are becoming philosophical. Wouldn't it be sweet if we all became better people after this?

Gregory Wouldn't it just.

Kate You don't seem convinced.

Gregory All I can see at the moment is the hurting.

Trixie That's quite natural. You're hurting too. And it's not over yet.

Kate Oh, jolly.

Colin But it will get better. It has to. Every one of us in this room cares about Amy. Yes, I know, Sylvia's care is a little confused at the moment. But we all care about Sylvia too. There is a solution to this situation. There has to be. And we'll find it.

Trixie Perhaps she needs to understand that asking for help is a sign of strength not of weakness.

Gregory We're not talking about a little neighbourly help. Oh, I don't mean to belittle what you and Kate have done for Amy, and for me for that matter. Had it not been for your kindness Amy would have had no normal life at all. But now it has reached a stage where Amy's whole life — and mine, and Sylvia's — rests on a decision for which there is no easy answer, if any answer at all. Whatever she chooses results in some degree of loss for someone.

Trixie Well, at the end of the day, it is her decision. No-one can judge her for it.

Gregory But they will. She will be judged as either foolish or heartless.

Trixie She must learn not to listen.

Colin I think she must listen to advice. I know she doesn't want Sylvia to leave her home. But if she was safe and well looked after Amy might learn to accept that it's for the best and find some peace for the future.

Gregory And then of course, she will judge herself. And if she finds that she is guilty of neglect or lack of love or cruelty, then it will all have been for nothing. And she will never be at peace.

Trixie Then you must help her find it — somehow.

Gregory I can't. She has to find it herself.

Kate Are well-read people always this depressing?

Colin Don't be facetious, Kate.

Kate I only asked. Because if so then I'll definitely stick to my glossies.

Trixie You would have done anyway, Kate dear. Don't blame this situation for your lack of culture.

Kate I am a child of my culture. I am one of the most cultural people I know.

Colin How on earth did you and Amy become friends?

Kate Attraction of opposites. Oh, I do wish she had at least opened her presents. Now everything is spoiled.

Trixie If you're going to get petulant, Kate, could you do us all a favour, and get there from some place other than here.

Kate What have I done now?

Trixie Colin, be an angel and take Kate out to play for a while.

Kate Am I going to miss anything terribly interesting?

Gregory I shouldn't think so, Kate.

Kate In that case, I think Trixie's suggestion has a lot to be said for it. What do you say, Colin?

Colin (*laughing*) All right, you win, but I'll come back later and see how Amy is and try to talk again.

Colin takes Kate's hand and leads her to the door

Come on, you. If I can cope with Aunt Sylvia as a passenger, I can certainly cope with you.

Kate I wouldn't be so sure about that!

Colin (*to Gregory*) See you soon.

Kate and Colin exit into the hall

Trixie (*moving to Gregory*) Now then, Gregory, I'm not one to desert a sinking ship, and I'll stay as long as I'm needed, but I felt that we were achieving very little at that particular general meeting. It required breaking up. Because it's Amy's life, and we can't decide for her.

Gregory I suppose not ...

Trixie Now the fact that you two were meant for each other seems obvious. But that doesn't immediately remove all the obstacles from your path. In that sense, Kate is right. Life can be a sod, sometimes. Ultimately you have to decide whether your love for Amy is strong enough to stand by her whatever happens. We talk about the right choice, the wrong choice. Amy may feel that she has no choice at all, but must stand by a decision when everything in her screams out against that decision. And she will not be able to see it through without you.

Gregory That sounds profound, Trixie, but I reckon your argument has a flaw in it somewhere.

Trixie It does. It means that there might not be a happy ending in sight. But would that stop you loving her?

Gregory Nothing in the world could do that.

Trixie In which case you're on much stronger ground. Because whatever the outcome you'll still love her. That won't have been wasted.

Gregory I can't help wondering what would have happened if we hadn't met.

Trixie You would not have loved each other, nor known what it was to be loved as you are. And that would indeed have been a waste. (*Pause*) And on that note I really must go before I become too sentimental for anyone's good. Call me if you need me. I'm only across the road.

Gregory What should I do?

Trixie Whatever is needed. (*She puts a hand on his shoulder*) Call me.

Trixie exits into the hall

Gregory stands in the centre of the room. He puts his head in his hands and for a moment he seems completely defeated. Then he lifts his head and looks around him. He looks at Sylvia asleep in the chair then goes to the bottom of the stairs

Gregory (*calling softly*) Amy? Amy? (*He turns back and looks at Sylvia*)

Sylvia stirs slightly

Gregory heads up the stairs

Sylvia opens her eyes. She looks around the room, disorientated

Sylvia Amy?

Hearing Sylvia, Gregory comes down the stairs again

Gregory It's all right, Sylvia. I'm here. Do you want anything? (*He goes to her side*)

Sylvia looks puzzled for a moment, then smiles and takes his hand

    I know you, don't I?
Gregory Yes. I'm Gregory.
Sylvia You came to tea.
Gregory Yes.
Sylvia You … You … Oh … How silly. You … (*She gestures at the bookcase*)
Gregory Books?
Sylvia (*delightedly*) Books!
Gregory Yes, I came to look at an old book. That's right. (*He sits on the sofa*)
Sylvia That's right, I know. (*Pause*) That other man?
Gregory What other man?
Sylvia The books. He wrote one. Her book.
Gregory Do you mean the book I came to see? *Ivanhoe*?
Sylvia That wasn't him.
Gregory Walter Scott wrote *Ivanhoe*.
Sylvia Yes. Clever man.
Gregory Yes.
Sylvia (*looking closely at Gregory*) That smile. I know. I knew before. I thought … Yes. That's him.
Gregory Who?
Sylvia That look. I saw it before, here. In this room. He looked at my sister. And I saw how he felt. And I thought, "Yes, that's how it is." Same look. Same face. And I know now too. You love her, don't you?
Gregory (*after a pause*) Yes. Yes I do love her.
Sylvia I've seen you, sometimes. I can see how it is. I've never — never loved like that. But I — know. I know what it is like to love someone. (*During the following she turns to face out into the audience and speaks almost to*

herself) Yes, I do. I had a little girl once. She wasn't mine. Not really mine, but I loved her as though she were mine. And so I suppose, in a way, she became mine. Do you see?

Gregory Yes.

Sylvia Feeling like that for someone else, it makes life good. Like a bright light shining through you. And laughter. It makes you want to laugh — out loud. And we laughed together. She had a beautiful laugh, my little girl. And sometimes you think that you will burst with the feeling. So you make yourself very small, to hold the feeling in, so that it will never leave you, and no-one will see that you want to cry with joy. (*She pauses, struggling with emotions, trying to make sense of something*) I miss her when she's away. It seems — such a long time — since I saw her. Sometimes I think that I see her — and then I don't know. It's very silly. But when you haven't seen someone for a long time — you begin to — forget — their face. Isn't that silly?

Gregory No. It's not silly.

Sylvia It's so hard — all the — forgetting. But it would be too much — to forget her. (*She turns to look at Gregory*) Have you seen her?

Gregory (*after a pause*) Yes.

Sylvia Tell me … Help me remember.

Gregory She has a lovely face. Some people might think it quite ordinary, but to you and me — it's beautiful.

Sylvia Oh, yes. Is it a happy face?

Gregory When she smiles, you see it first in her eyes. And then it breaks over her whole face.

Sylvia What colour are her eyes?

Gregory Grey.

Sylvia Yes, yes, I remember. And her hair?

Gregory Brown.

Sylvia And long down her back.

Gregory She had it cut. It's shorter now.

Sylvia Is it?

Gregory Yes.

Sylvia When did she cut it?

Gregory (*after a pause*) I don't know. Some time ago I think.

Sylvia No. No. I don't remember … And I'd so like to remember once more — before … Why did she go?

Gregory She didn't go anywhere, Sylvia.

Sylvia Did something happen to her?

Gregory In a way. But nothing bad.

Gregory suddenly moves to Sylvia and takes her hands

(*Quickly but kindly*) Listen, Sylvia. Let me help you to remember. The little girl that you loved didn't leave you. She didn't go away. She just grew up. And she became a beautiful, warm, caring young woman who still loves you very much. But for a while you couldn't remember her face. Then one day I came here and I met Amy. And we fell in love.

Sylvia You fell in love — with Amy?

Gregory Can you blame me?

Sylvia No. No, of course not.

Gregory Amy is really very fortunate. She has been loved twice, in a way that very few are ever loved.

Sylvia (*thoughtfully*) No — no — not Amy.

Gregory Yes.

Sylvia No. It is we who are the lucky ones.

Gregory (*relieved*) Yes. Yes, we are.

Sylvia Is she happy?

Gregory She's … She's worried. About you.

Sylvia She has no need to worry about me. (*She gets up and begins to walk to the bottom of the stairs*) She mustn't. No need.

Gregory (*standing*) I suppose we always worry for the people we love. It's an occupational hazard.

Sylvia (*laughing*) I don't know what you mean. I expect I did. Once. (*She turns to look at him*) You've been very kind. Thank you for helping me — to remember.

Gregory Are you all right?

Sylvia I'm — tired.

Gregory Can I call — anyone?

Sylvia No. No. (*She looks up the stairs and then seems unsure what to do as though she has forgotten where she was going. She turns and looks around the room, then moves to the desk and looks at the jigsaw box lid*) It is a lovely face, isn't it?

Gregory Whose?

Amy enters slowly down the stairs, reaching the bottom at the end of Sylvia's next speech

Sylvia The lady. It's very clever. You can put it together any time you want to. Put it all together — and there she is. And it helps you — remember. All those little bits of blue. Lovely brown hair.

Gregory (*seeing Amy*) Amy?

Sylvia looks up and sees Amy. They look at one another. Sylvia walks towards Amy. She puts out her hand and touches Amy's cheek and smiles

Sylvia Yes. Altogether. (*She kisses Amy's cheek, then sighs*) I'm so — tired.
(*She walks past Amy and begins to climb the stairs*)
Amy (*looking at Gregory*) What happened?
Gregory She asked me and I — helped her remember.
Amy (*incredulously*) You told her?
Gregory Yes.
Amy Why?
Gregory Perhaps it was for me, because I could not bear the thought of life without you. Or perhaps it was for you because you needed to find yourself again. Or perhaps it was for Sylvia, because of all her memories the loss of her child's face seemed the hardest to lose. Or perhaps I did it because the moment seemed right and it was the only thing I could have done. I don't know.
Amy What did she say?
Gregory She said "Thank you."
Amy Did she understand? I mean, really understand?
Gregory In that moment I think she did, yes. I think she understood a great deal.
Amy Do you think she'll remember now? Do you think she'll know me?
Gregory Who can say? But I want you to remember something. She told me how much she loves you. It was — beautiful. And something like that can't just disappear into nothing. I want you to hold on to it. In that moment she knew you, and remembered everything that had ever been important to her.
Amy That's what's so sad. I've seen it in her eyes sometimes. She knows what she's losing. It must be so frightening to look forward and see — nothing ... Just emptiness.
Gregory What do you see, Amy, when you look forward?
Amy I don't know. I wonder if I dare look. Sometimes it looks empty for me too. And that's worse than not looking. A sort of dying. But I know what I want to see.
Gregory The day we first met you said that you wanted to be part of an ever-flowing stream. To look into the future and see a part of yourself there.
Amy Something like that.
Gregory I want to share that with you, if you'd let me.
Amy (*turning to him, then taking his hand and leading him to the window*) Will you lie under the skylight and look at the stars with me?
Gregory I'd count them for you if you asked me.
Amy That's impossible.

They look out of the window, Gregory standing behind Amy with his arms around her

Gregory Who knows. One day it might not be. One day there will be honeymoon trips to Venus and I'll be able to inscribe the whole of *Ivanhoe* on the inside of a gold ring, and you'll be able to read it at the touch of a button.

Amy It will give me something to do while you're counting the stars.

Gregory One day there may be a medical breakthrough to help people like Sylvia.

Amy Do you think that's possible?

Gregory They say it might. Who knows. It might be a long wait. But then again, it might not be so long. It might be happening in some laboratory as we speak. Think of that.

Amy Yes, think of that. (*Pause*) I ought to go and see if she's all right.

Gregory Not just yet. I think she needs time on her own too.

Amy She forgets so easily. I don't want her to be frightened. I ought to go and check. Don't go away. I'll be right back. (*She moves away*) Oh look. My birthday cake. We didn't even cut it.

Gregory Do you want to?

Amy I don't know. It's a child's cake. And I'm forty years old.

Gregory Well, you know what they say about being forty. It's when life begins. (*He sits on the sofa*) That red rug I mentioned is still in the car. We could swap grapes for chocolate cake.

Amy There's no-one to sit with Sylvia.

Gregory Well, I could bring it in here and we could spread it out below the window and pretend ... Oh no, on second thoughts, we might be interrupted. Colin said he'd come back and see how you are, and I presume Kate will come with him. She had that look in her eye that says she's not going to let go very easily. And to be honest, it's not that big a rug.

Amy Oh well. We could always suggest they watch *War and Peace*. Kate's never seen it, you know.

Gregory Is that so?

They laugh. Amy sits beside Gregory on the sofa and he kisses her

Oh, Amy. Look forward with me? Please grow old with me. The best is yet to be.

Gregory takes Amy's face in his hands. She looks up at him

They look towards a future in which surely they must be together, despite all the unknowns

The Everly Brothers sing "Let It Be Me"

The Lights fade, leaving a spotlight on Gregory and Amy. Then the spotlight fades to Black-out

CURTAIN

FURNITURE AND PROPERTY LIST

ACT I
SCENE 1

On stage: Large bookcase with many books
Armchair
Sofa
Small coffee table
Sideboard. *On it*: books including *Ivanhoe* with uncut pages
Desk. *On it*: telephone, blotter, writing materials
Desk chair. *On it*: **Sylvia**'s cardigan
CD player
Selection of CDs
Glossy magazine for **Kate**

Off stage: Two carrier bags containing hardback second-hand books (**Amy**)
Tray of tea things including cake (**Kate**)
Plates (**Sylvia**)

Personal: **Kate**: watch (worn throughout)

SCENE 2

Set: Jigsaw puzzle in box on desk
Shopping list on desk

Strike: Tea things
Carrier bags

Off stage: Bowl of cereal and spoon (**Amy**)

SCENE 3

Re-set: Close window curtains

Set: Fashion magazine for **Kate**

Strike: Cereal bowl and spoon
Jigsaw puzzle

Off stage: Glass of milk (**Kate**)

ACT II
SCENE 1

On stage: As Act I
Happy birthday banner
Hooks for balloons
Vacuum cleaner (practical) for **Amy**
On coffee table: newspaper
On desk: bag of balloons, inflated balloons tied together with string,
    Ivanhoe
On sideboard: pile of plates and paper napkins

Off stage: Bottle of champagne in gift bag (**Gregory**)
Bags of shopping (**Trixie**)
Birthday cake (**Kate**)
Plate of sausages (**Kate**)
Tray of drinks (**Kate**)
Plates of sandwiches and biscuits (**Colin**)
Chocolate cake with candles, box of matches, cake knife (**Trixie**)

SCENE 2

Strike: All party food except cake

Set: Drink for **Kate**

LIGHTING PLOT

ACT I, Scene 1

To open: General interior lighting with afternoon setting on window backing

No cues

ACT I, Scene 2

To open: General interior lighting with morning setting on window backing

No cues

ACT I, Scene 3

To open: General interior lighting with night-time setting on window backing

No cues

ACT II, Scene 1

To open: General interior lighting with afternoon setting on window backing

No cues

ACT II, Scene 2

To open: General interior lighting with afternoon setting on window backing

Cue 1   Music: the Everly Brothers   (Page 61)
            Fade lights to spotlight on **Gregory** *and* **Amy***;*
            then black-out

EFFECTS PLOT

The music to be used is *Let It Be Me* by the Everly Brothers written by Curtis/Becaud/Delanoe published 1960 by Cadence records ref.1376.

ACT I

ACT II